THE
Healing
ART
OF
Encouragement

THE *Healing* ART OF

While this book is designed for the reader's personal enjoyment and profit, it is also intended for group study. A Leader's Guide with Victor Multiuse Transparency Masters is available from your local bookstore or from the publisher.

VICTOR BOOKS ®

A DIVISION OF SCRIPTURE PRESS PUBLICATIONS INC.
USA CANADA ENGLAND

Encouragement

DAVID W. AYCOCK

Recommended Dewey Decimal
Classification: 248
Suggested Subject Heading: CHRISTIAN
LIFE; HUMAN RELATIONS

Library of Congress Catalog Card
Number: 87-81022
ISBN: 0-89693-350-4

For information, address Victor Books,
P.O. Box 1825, Wheaton, Illinois 60189.

Contents

*To my loving wife, LeNan,
who encourages me daily with
thoughtful words and loving
actions.*

Preface

This volume is a practical guide to the art of encouragement. It is designed to provide instructions to Christians on how they can encourage one another. I have made an effort to meld biblical and psychological principles for a comprehensive treatment of the topic. Examples are provided liberally to enhance skill acquisition.

The book is organized to demonstrate the need for encouragement and to provide the practical instruction needed to fill this need. A discussion of the pervasiveness of discouragement in our world and a general introduction to the topic of encouragement comprise the first two chapters. The following six chapters describe the methods we should use to carry out encouragement: listening, responding, offering compliments and feedback, motivating others, backing encouraging words with actions, and celebrating victories. Chapter 9 provides guidelines for *accepting* encouragement. Chapters 10 and 11 describe the use of encouragement in the special cases of parenting and counseling. The final chapter discusses the biblical mandate that Christians incorporate encouragement into their lifestyles.

Encouragement is presented as a necessary and rewarding resource available to everyone. However, it is not presented as a quick fix to patch up friendships or as an easy three-step method to happiness. Instead, encouragement is seen as a powerful relationship skill which can be learned through the application and practice of well-documented principles. Encouragement should never be thought of as a phony way to offer praise or compliments. You will see the word *realistic* used repeatedly herein to emphasize the importance of honesty in all interactions with others.

I have chosen to use a personal writing style in order to incorporate many of my own experiences as both a dispenser and recipient of encouragement. In the examples taken from my professional practice of psychology, identities have been altered to protect the confidentiality of those persons with whom I have worked.

I trust this volume will enhance your spiritual growth and teach you the vital skills needed to encourage others. Read it prayerfully and practice it daily.

1.

Discouragement Has Us Surrounded

"In all these things we are more than conquerors through Him who loved us" (Romans 8:37).

How do you feel after watching the evening news? You've just been treated to a half hour of gloom. The economy's down. There's a volatile situation in the Middle East. Someone has committed a heinous crime. The weather is not cooperating with the farmers and prices may rise. And if the news isn't bad enough, advertisers have told you that you're not using the right painkiller and that your car is outmoded. Discouraging, isn't it?

How do you feel when you leave your church service? Your pastor may have delivered a marvelous sermon. Perhaps he emphasized important spiritual truths and tied biblical passages together masterfully. But if you're honest with yourself, you'll probably admit that you're not practicing all of those biblical behaviors. When you stack yourself up next to Jesus Christ, of course you fall short—everyone does. But you feel inferior even when you compare yourself with fellow church members. Is it discouraging?

11

How do you feel after you spend some time with a Christian friend? You talked about the local ball team and about the new building going up downtown. You discussed the problem of finding affordable baby-sitters. You even talked about how nice the last Sunday service was at church. But you never shared your *real* feelings—the positive or negative ones. You want to be balanced, you know. Do you feel discouraged?

Many Christians would likely answer, "Yes, I really am discouraged!" It's discouraging to hear negative reports on the evening newscast. It's discouraging to compare ourselves unfavorably with others. It's discouraging to spend time with friends and never share our important personal feelings.

A DISCOURAGED WORLD

Discouragement and pessimism thrive in our society. A recent poll of grammar school children found that a majority of the students believed that they would not live to old age. Economists predict a myriad of financial disasters around the globe. World leaders disagree on practically every issue. Corruption is so widespread that we dare not trust anyone we don't know.

This discouragement is not surprising. Scripture describes God's creation as being frustrated and in "bondage to decay" (Rom. 8:20-21). Christ Himself warned that wars and natural disasters would be commonplace before He returned (Matt. 24:4-8). However, many Christians are just as discouraged as the non-Christians. Believers are pessimistic and worry about everything from how God will intervene in world politics to how they'll be accepted by the other members of their Sunday School class. Merely telling Christians to stop fretting and trust God is not enough.

Alan was a discouraged Christian. He had made a profession of faith in Christ when he was young and now he was in college. Even though he was making good grades in pursuit of a potentially lucrative business career, he was down and lacked motivation to take care of his basic needs. When Alan came to see me, he was noticeably depressed. He was unsure of his future. He related his concerns about nuclear war and the economy, and he wondered if all of his study and preparation for a career was a wasted effort. Alan knew that God is in control of world politics, but he still felt discouraged. He had tried to snap out of it and think biblical thoughts, but this never seemed to work for very long. He wanted to share his faith with others, but he feared that people would question His Christian commitment. So he "played the game" at church and around his Christian friends, but deep down inside Alan was hurting.

I could have tried to assure Alan that God was capable of taking care of him and that he should believe this and become happier. But Alan did not need to be convinced of God's omnipotence. He was well-versed in the doctrine of God. He needed to learn to incorporate his knowledge into experience through the mutual encouragement that should be available within the body of Christ. Alan needed training in encouragement.

DISCOURAGEMENT: A WAY OF LIFE

Even though encouragement is an effective way to build self-esteem and emotional well-being, it is not widely practiced in our society. Discouragement begins when we're young. In school, teachers inevitably scored my papers by *subtracting* points for incorrect answers. Red markings on test papers rarely complimented the correct answers. Instead of "Good Job" or "That's a thoughtful point," teachers' comments were usually negative and discouraging.

Our law enforcement system is quite discouraging as well. Many of us feel anxious when we see a patrolman even if we aren't breaking the law. We are rarely commended for lawful behaviors, just punished for unlawful ones.

In our close relationships, discouragement is often the rule. Spouses find it easy to offer criticism of each other's driving or cooking, but rarely remember to reinforce a job well done. Parents readily reprimand their children for tracking mud into the house or spilling their milk, but they forget to thank the children when they wipe their feet outside or drink their milk without spilling a drop. Parishioners criticize church members who don't attend services regularly and label them uncommitted, but they rarely encourage those who do come each week. Yes, discouragement abounds in our world.

HELPLESSNESS

When people are subjected to a constant diet of discouragement, they begin to feel helpless and resourceless. Researcher Martin Seligman has done extensive work identifying a syndrome he calls "learned helplessness."[1] Seligman subjected laboratory dogs to electric shock without any possibility for their escape. At first the dogs reacted with much excitability to the electric current, but they soon learned to absorb it passively since their excitable responses were not effective in turning off the punishment.

After these animals had been conditioned to be passive, Seligman placed them in a laboratory apparatus which had an electric grid on one-half and a non-electric floor on the other. The passive dogs were placed on the electric side of the apparatus and the current was turned on. The animals passively absorbed the shock. Other dogs were introduced to the experiment who had never been conditioned to be passive. When the shock was applied, these normal dogs quickly ran to the neutral area but the passive dogs did not follow their lead. In fact, the researchers had to use tremendous force to pull these reluctant passive dogs away from the painful electric current to the neutral area.

These animals had learned to be helpless. They were taught that their reactions made no difference, so these discouraged animals quit reacting. In the same way, people who are discouraged again and again, particularly when they are young, often come to believe that they are helpless to effect any changes in their lives. They lack motivation to try new things and instantly give up whenever an obstacle is encountered. They have poor self-esteem and do not see themselves as having any capabilities to perform adequately for themselves or for God. They do not feel resourceful and usually will not improve unless they are retrained through very consistently encouraging persons.

Encouragers can make an enormous impact upon persons who perceive themselves as helpless. Renee is a case in point. She was raised in an urban housing project. She was one of seven children and she never met her father. Her mother was an unskilled laborer who worked from time to time and left Renee's 13-year-old sister in charge of the household.

Without social status, financial advantages, or adequate parenting, Renee learned at an early age that she didn't count. She was at the mercy of a mother who saw her children as a burden, and an older sister who developed household policies to suit her own inconsistent whims. Not surprisingly, Renee developed feelings of learned helplessness and seemed to lack even the slightest ambition.

I met Renee at Sunday School when she was 10 years old. I was in college and a friend, Dawn, knew Renee through a student teaching assignment. Dawn was an exceptional encourager. She spent time with Renee, nurturing her spiritually and mirroring God's love. Dawn taught Renee important social skills and engineered success experiences that further strengthened Renee's feelings of resourcefulness.

Renee learned that she was somebody and that she could impact her world positively. Her self-esteem grew tremendously and she became an important encourager to her younger siblings. Encouragement and love had conquered learned helplessness.

SELF-INDUCED DISCOURAGEMENT

Discouragement often catches us off guard. We all know people who are highly critical and we usually keep our distance from them. Even when they are closely related to us, we find many ways to stay away from them. But these folks aren't the only sources of discouragement. In fact, more often than not, we are our own worst discouragers. We compare ourselves unfavorably with others or exaggerate our faults and catastrophize the consequences of perceived personal inadequacies. Discouragement saps our energy and trounces our motivation as we often develop a "who cares" attitude. We feel that we will never measure up, so why should we even try?

Required Personal Perfectionism. Perhaps the greatest source of self-induced discouragement is the perfection we require of ourselves. Often we set grandiose goals for ourselves and expect perfect performances on virtually every task. When we fail (and we often do), we feel discouraged. Others may try to help us gain a realistic perspective, but we quickly discount their attempts at encouragement by reasoning that they are really insincere or are merely pampering us.

Our perfectionistic perspective allows us to be encouraging to others, but we can't extend the same courtesy to ourselves. We might say "nice try" when someone else drops a pass, but we berate ourselves loudly and often when we do the same thing. People often feel sorry for us at first and try to console us. But our constant self-abasement tires them and they either stay away from us or accept our assessments of our own worthlessness and, in the end, agree with us.

Fred was a discouraged young man. He was a college student in a rigorous course of study in a very difficult major. Fred had gone through high school on a steady diet of A's and he could not deal with these "substandard" college grades. Comparisons with other students who were also performing in his range was little consolation to Fred because he considered their performances to be the best they could do. However, he *knew* he could do much better. Fred's problem was not unfavorable comparison with others, but rather unfavorable performance for his personal standards. In fact, I could see that he probably *did* have the ability to make A's, but his self-imposed pressure was preventing this.

Our work focused on the realistic assessment of his abilities and the demands he was under. Once Fred "lightened up" on himself, the A's came more easily. We worked long hours on this realistic perception of himself and Fred soon stopped discouraging himself. He was able to enjoy his college preparation and actually graduated with honors once he quit requiring personal perfection.

Perfectionism and Stress. The need for perfection in an imperfect world can be a severe handicap. Having to do all things perfectly produces excess stress. To the perfectionist, winning is all that matters. The way one plays the game is of little consequence except as it affects the outcome. This, of course, places the perfectionist under constant pressure to perform and allows him no excuses for mistakes.

Sources of Perfectionism. Perfectionism may arise in a number of ways. Many adopt a perfectionistic stance in order to compensate for feared inadequacies. They reason that they are inadequate in an area of their lives and that this inadequacy carries tremendous negative consequences. Therefore, they must insure success in this perceived inadequate area at any cost in order to break even. Compensation is a common reaction among perfectionists.

Another source of perfectionism may be personal arrogance. The arrogant perfectionist reasons that it may be permissible for others to be imperfect, but he believes that he is somehow better. He pits himself against the world, accepting nothing but complete success in every venture in order to maintain positive self-esteem and satisfaction with life.

When I think of a person whose perfectionism stems from this cause, I am often reminded of Jesus' conversation with a rich, young ruler (Matt. 19:16-22). The young man asked Jesus how he might inherit eternal life. It sounds like a good opportunity for soul-winning when a willing individual goes to Christ Himself and requests the steps he must take to go to heaven. Yet after this man talked with Jesus, he walked away sadly and apparently failed to gain eternal life.

What was the problem? Had Jesus made an error in His dealings with this young man? No, the young man made a conscious choice to leave which did not reflect any error on Jesus' part. A successful conversion was not the result of this encounter. If this can happen to our Lord, clearly it can happen to us. It is the height of arrogance for us to believe that we are immune from disappointing personal experiences. No one can control the world and especially the behavior of others.

It would seem that the inevitable imperfections that arise in the arrogant perfectionist's life would quickly frustrate him and cause him to abandon this standard. Quite the opposite is the case. Encountered imperfections serve only to motivate the arrogant perfectionist more strongly to conquer the world. These attitudes may create difficulties in his ability to rely on God's strength and power.

Perfectionism may also arise from the exaggerated estimates of the consequences of one's failures. The motivation for this perfectionist is not arrogance, but rather fear that imperfect performance will result in ultimate doom. People with this attitude are usually "nervous wrecks" who constantly dread the failure lurking right around the corner which (they believe) will assuredly create tremendous personal upheaval. This perfectionism is an attempt to stay one step ahead of a horrible fate. It produces a constant state of distress.

A fellow student in my college residence hall was this type of perfectionist. He worried constantly about errors which he might make in the future: assignments that he would botch or social relationships that he would somehow cause to sour. He was very successful in almost all of his pursuits, but he never seemed to really enjoy life. He believed that he was just escaping catastrophe after catastrophe.

Catastrophism is a common theme that arises in counseling. People don't want to teach Sunday School because they think their classes will laugh them to scorn or make fun of their nervousness. Students fear taking an exam because they envision themselves flunking out of school if they can't answer some question. People shy away from introducing themselves to others for fear that they will not be seen as good conversationalists and this will assuredly result in social leprosy.

These perceptions obviously seem exaggerated and out of line with reality. Certainly people with these ideas need to develop more realistic views of their circumstances and the probable results of their actions. But often it is not easy to convince a catastrophist of his irrationality simply by presenting rational facts. An effective treatment for these perfectionists is to prescribe the very failure that they so desperately dread. I have often suggested to a fearful public speaker that he trip on the way to the podium, so he could discover for himself that this imperfection would not result in the terrible consequences he had imagined. In fact, these purposeful small imperfections often free people up tremendously because after one has erred, it is impossible to do a perfect job. Now he can concentrate on doing merely a good job. This is a more manageable task.

Perfectionism can also provide a convenient excuse for those who do not wish to attempt a difficult task. The logic goes like this: "Since it must be done right (perfectly) and I can't insure that, I won't attempt it at all." This type of perfectionism is paralyzing.

Christine was a perfectionist who used this cop-out regularly. She was 35 years old and worked for a Christian organization. Christine consulted me because she had never been married and was beginning to wonder if she ever would find a mate. She was quite lonely and somewhat depressed.

As we began to investigate her interpersonal behaviors, it became obvious that Christine was making little effort to place herself in the social arena. She never attended the singles functions at her local church and associated almost exclusively with married women. When confronted about this lack of contact with men, she reported, "I never know the right (perfect) thing to say to guys, so I just stay away from them."

Clearly, Christine's strategy was not effective in meeting her stated desire (a close relationship with a man). Her belief that she had to say the perfect thing and act the perfect way around men effectively prevented her from making any attempts at interaction with them at all. We worked diligently at changing her perfectionistic internal monologues and practicing pro-social behaviors around men.

Whatever the source of perfectionism, its outworkings in our lives usually result in crippling discouragement. And we have only ourselves to blame. As Pogo said, "We have met the enemy and he is us." This self-imposed discouragement must be first recognized and then modified. Encouragement is the treatment of choice to counteract this emotional menace.

Discouragement sometimes arises from subjection to powerful forces which prevent individual control and train persons to be helpless. However, much more frequently discouragement is self-induced. We demand perfection of ourselves and compare ourselves unfavorably with those around us. Discouragement saps our energy and leaves us unmotivated and unhappy. Encouraging others is the most effective antidote to this significant problem.

2.
What Is Encouragement?

"Therefore encourage one another and build each other up, just as in fact you are doing" (1 Thessalonians 5:11).

When you think about encouragement, what ideas come to your mind? Perhaps you picture the wise fathers in old television shows consoling their sons after some misbehavior. There's Ward Cleaver patting the Beaver on the head after a long, comforting talk, or Sheriff Andy Taylor promising little Opie a brighter day tomorrow. Or perhaps you think of a coach on the sidelines encouraging his athletes to perform to their potential.

The Bible is a rich repository of encouraging illustrations as well. Fatherly encouragement following misbehavior is clearly demonstrated as the prodigal son was welcomed home after squandering his resources on disgraceful living. Joshua urged his troops into battle, and the Apostle Paul gave pep talks about running a good race and finishing the course. Jesus built confidence in His discouraged disciple by assigning Peter a leadership position just after the apostle failed miserably in upholding allegiance to his Lord.

Perhaps you think of examples such as these or maybe your own encouraging experiences. My most constant encourager throughout life has been my mother. She has nurtured me, believed in me, disciplined me, and built my confidence. She continuously shows support and stimulates me to further growth and success. She's a great encourager.

Encouragement encompasses all the behaviors in these illustrations. It's the forgiving attitude of the prodigal's father and the pat on the head by Ward Cleaver that demonstrates acceptance and helps us develop and grow. It's the stimulation to action by General Joshua and the urging and inspiring of Paul and the athletic coach to produce to our potential. It's the nurturing and discipline loving mothers use to point us in the right direction. And it's the building of confidence by Jesus who helps us recognize our strengths instead of focusing on weaknesses. It is *not* blind acceptance of any behavior, a barrage of phony compliments for every action, or a patronizing pat on the back without regard for a person's real feelings.

When others encourage us, we feel good about ourselves. We feel good about the encourager. We are willing to try new things and our confidence increases. Encouraged people are effective people. They have positive self-esteem and expect success in the tasks they undertake. They tend to have positive relationships with others and can concentrate on helping others rather than on their own personal inadequacies. Furthermore, encouraged people are the best encouragers of others!

Not surprisingly, encouragement holds a prominent place in the Scriptures as an adaptive human resource. In the Book of Acts, Luke routinely reports that encouragement was a central aspect of the missionary ventures of the early apostles. Encouragement is numbered among the "spiritual gifts" and exhortations for Christians to build one another up are legion. The motivational potential of encouragement is clearly understood by God and communicated to His church.

Consider your own experience with encouragement. Can you recall a personal situation in which someone gave you sincere positive feedback on your performance? It feels uplifting for a person to notice your work in the first place. Then when they comment positively, it gives you a feeling of accomplishment and recognition that you have really impacted the world in a favorable manner. You tend to cherish thcse encouraging words and recall them the next time you are faced with that task or a similar one.

I recall my early experiences with public speaking. A recent poll identified this action as the most feared common stressor of Americans, and I was no exception. Speaking in front of groups of people, even those I knew personally, frightened me terribly. It made me sweat and clouded my thinking to the extent that I couldn't concentrate on anything but my anxiety.

In my sophomore year of college I took on a major in theology to compliment my psychology major. Little did I know what I was getting into. Churches are quite attracted to aspiring theologians and pounce on them with invitations to speak. I was in double jeopardy because my father is a pastor who had no qualms about proffering these invitations to me. So I was off to the races!

My early sermons were filled with redundancies and well-worn examples and admonitions, but the parishioners encouraged me. My father recognized my many glaring weaknesses, but reinforced my positive qualities and encouraged me to continue speaking publicly by offering his pulpit regularly.

Soon I began to gain some confidence. I lost many of my earlier fears, such as losing my composure, going completely blank, or saying something stupid. I was learning to focus on the material I was teaching instead of on my anxiety.

By the time I reached graduate school, I felt rather comfortable speaking in front of groups. I earned a graduate teaching assistantship in my first year and this placed me in a position to sharpen my skills. I first assisted an advanced graduate student who added a new twist to the encouragement of my public speaking. He critiqued my performance and not only highlighted my strengths, but pointed out deficiencies and encouraged me to improve in these areas. The next year I assisted a wise professor who also provided me with speaking opportunities and continued the critical evaluation. He too emphasized my strengths as well as my weaknesses and told me how to correct my errors. This was enormously encouraging and helped me hone my speaking skills and gain even more confidence. My progress was further encouraged by the graduate department entrusting me with senior instructor duties for my own graduate course and providing me with an assistant whom I could encourage.

Now I speak regularly to groups ranging from a handful to hundreds. I give seminars, lecture to college classes, lead group discussions, and conduct training workshops. My comfort in front of groups and skills in public speaking are a result of arduous work spurred by a progression of encouragements from others. First came the encouragement to take risks I feared and continual urging to persevere even though my performance was far from perfect. Then people encouraged the strengths they saw and, finally, I was provided with critical and honest feedback with suggestions for improvement. Given this encouraging environment, success was all but assured.

DIVINE ENCOURAGEMENT

Though we usually think of encouragement in terms of human interaction, God's encouragement must not be overlooked. The Lord has provided us with a means of justification through His Son and promises of His constant concern for us. Besides these encouraging truths, God's encouragement often instills the confidence we need to take on His work. This practical outworking of God's encouragement is exemplified clearly in the life of Ezra the priest. This biblical writer led many of his fellow Jews from their exile in Babylon back to Jerusalem to rebuild the temple. Though he had permission from the king of Persia for this task, he encountered constant resistance to the building and relocation operations. It would have been very easy for Ezra to become discouraged. However, Ezra exclaimed, "Because the hand of the Lord my God was on me, I took courage and gathered leading men from Israel to go up with me" (Ezra 7:28). The encouragement Ezra received from God translated into service for the Lord's ministry.

Sometimes God's encouragement provides us with the motivation to persevere in difficult and trying circumstances. Indeed, this is the theme of many of the psalms. King David often surveyed the state of affairs in his world and discovered that things were not equitable. He witnessed unfairness in his dealings with Saul and his own family as well as in the lives of his countrymen and God's enemies. Psalm 10 illustrates the despair experienced by the author as he asks, "Why, O Lord, do You stand far off? Why do You hide Yourself in times of trouble?" (v. 1) Then after expressing the unfairness exhibited daily by the ungodly, David reports, "You hear, O Lord, the desire of the afflicted; You *encourage* them, and You listen to their cry" (v. 17).

As a psychologist I meet regularly with persons who are exposed to unusual stressors and who are asked to carry heavy burdens. Often I do not understand why negative events like deaths, illnesses, and financial reverses are distributed so frequently to some and so rarely to others. Indeed, it does not seem fair. But I have also witnessed the encouragement that the Lord proffers to many in their time of despair. I marvel at the enabling strength to survive that

God's encouragement provides.

Empowerment, another purpose of God's encouragement, allows us to encourage others and in this way strengthen needy members in Christ's body. The Apostle Paul discusses this in 2 Corinthians 1:3-4:

> Praise be to God the Father of our Lord Jesus Christ, the Father of compassion and the God of all comfort, who comforts us in all our troubles, so that we can comfort those in any trouble with the comfort we ourselves have received from God.

Apparently, God allows distress to enter our lives at some points and then encourages us in these experiences so we can mirror His encouragement to others who are struggling with similar issues.

Susan was a wonderful example of this human transmission of God's encouragement. She met personal tragedy when her 15-year-old son was killed by a drunken motorist. She experienced every negative emotion imaginable, ranging from heartbreaking grief over her son's death to intense anger and hatred toward the murderer and the judicial system which dealt so lightly with him. As the months passed, Susan's grief for her son gave way to the hatred she felt for his assailant. Completely consumed with anger, Susan's relationships and other life tasks became secondary concerns. Her spiritual commitment waned as well. After months of experiencing this personal hell, she sought counseling to escape her anguish.

Needless to say, my attempts to understand Susan's pain were feeble at best since my children were alive and safe. But slowly she allowed me into portions of her world as she shared her constant pain and anger. Not long after therapy began, Susan announced a momentous decision. She reported that her current strategy of hatred and anger was maladaptive in that it disrupted all her life activities, further separated her from God, and did nothing to bring her son back to life. She stated that she wanted to forgive the man responsible for killing her son.

Immediately I was wary of her proposal as I feared that it was a quick fix to remove all her problems—a strategy ultimately doomed for failure and further despair. However, she soon had my approval as she shared her reasoning. Susan's previous attempts to be a "good Christian" and forgive this man had been short-lived and had instilled even more anger because she could not convince herself that he *deserved* her forgiveness. Now she wanted to forgive him because *she deserved* to be free from this albatross hanging around her neck. It was bad enough that this man had killed her son. Susan would not allow him to kill her as well.

This forgiveness was a tall order and it was only through God's grace and comfort that this process could even begin. Susan's new resolve gave her a framework within which she could accept God's encouragement. After struggling through the process over more months, Susan learned to forgive and picked up her life again. But this time she lived with more resolve and became involved in positive pursuits to deal with the drinking and driving issue. Through her political and community action, Susan was exposed to other parents who had suffered similar fates. She became the best counselor available to them as she empathized with their pain and pushed for a resolve to forgive. Then she encouraged them through the process with the comfort she had herself received from the Lord.

INTERPERSONAL BENEFITS

Encouragement is one of the most potent ways to endear ourselves to others. God created us for fellowship and we thrive on positive relationships with others. Encouragement is a social magnet because it is much in demand and short in supply. When we possess this resource, others seek us out and enjoy spending time with us. They want to be around us and include us in their social plans. They enjoy sharing their successes with us; they also turn to us in times of emotional need.

During my college years, I worked in a small community church on the weekends. Here I met Miss Greenway, a woman who had devoted her life to encouraging others. Miss Greenway was well into her seventies when I met her. She lived next door to the church with another elderly lady and attended church services regularly. Miss Greenway's pleasant demeanor and encouraging support were apparent to me almost immediately. She often invited me to her home after services and encouraged me in my academic work.

I did not fully appreciate Miss Greenway's influence, however, until I began visiting local residents and inviting them to church. Often I was met with coldness and disinterest until I identified the location of the church and mentioned Miss Greenway's house next door. Her name alone would change the tone of the encounter and melt some of the ice.

From the residents of the community I learned that Miss Greenway had been a Bible teacher in the local schools for years and was loved by practically everyone. People reported how encouraging she had been to them and how her kindness had affected them positively. Indeed, just by knowing Miss Greenway *I* was receiving interpersonal benefits from her lifelong work of encouragement.

Encouraging others is not just another good idea. It is a biblical mandate. The New Testament Epistles are filled with exhortations to encourage and build one another up. And just as is the case in the practice of other biblical directives, encouraging others provides numerous benefits to the encourager. These go well beyond the spiritual benefits accompanying obedience.

A word of caution is warranted here. Encouragement is a potent method of attracting others to us. As such, it has the potential for abuse. Encouraging words delivered insincerely to manipulate others are exploitive and often harmful. Buttering someone up with flattery to extract a favor is both dishonest and self-serving. Likewise, offering a compliment merely to have one reciprocated is a misuse of this resource. The appropriate use of encouragement is guided by a pure motive. Interpersonal benefits that result from our sincerity are welcomed and refreshing.

STRESS-REDUCTION BENEFITS

Encouragement is an important aspect of stress management. Encouragement we receive from others bolsters our confidence in our coping skills. This, in turn, usually translates into adaptive coping behaviors. There is a good deal of psychological research which demonstrates the value of positive personal perceptions as a stress moderator.[2]

The stress-reducing aspect of encouragement which is often overlooked is in the area of social support. Since encouragement is a social resource that attracts others to us, it follows that encouragers typically enjoy numerous friendships and supportive family relationships. Researchers have demonstrated a strong relationship between social support and effective coping. Lack of social support has been linked to problems as diverse as tuberculosis, alcoholism, schizophrenia, accident proneness, and suicide. Conversely, meaningful relationships with others have been found both to prevent stress and to moderate its consequences.

The social support networks of encouragers aid in the management of stress in several important ways. We gain emotional support from others which helps us realize that we're cared for and loved. We feel like we belong to the group and can share our stress with other people who care about us. We bear burdens for others in our social networks as well and recognize the important part we play in their lives and well-being. Others also provide us with the corrective feedback about our actions which helps us modify our coping strategies when appropriate.

An interesting illustration of the positive effects of close social support networks comes from a study of the Roseto, Pennsylvania community in the mid-1960s.[3] Roseto was an Italian community characterized by very "close-knit" families who were mutually supportive, gregarious, respectful of the elderly, and inclined to use the family as as resource for problem-solving. In comparison with other communities, Roseto citizens didn't diet or exercise more, nor did they smoke or drink less; yet their incidence of coronary heart disease was far less than the statistical average. This difference in illness rates was attributed to the stress-reduction benefits of their encouraging social support networks. After the original study of the Roseto population, the youths began to expanded their contacts, marrying outside of the Roseto community. As the close social networks began to disappear, the illness rates slowly increased to match those of the population at large.

Other studies have shown that the encouraging social support networks reduce work stress and enhance job success and satisfaction. One researcher found that persons trying to stop smoking were much more successful if they had encouraging support.[4] Encouragement creates strong relationships which we use as safety valves and vehicles of escape in times of stress.

This kind of mutual encouragement characterized the early churches described in the Book of Acts. The Jewish authorities were regularly persecuting the Christians, punishing them with physical beatings and even death. These stressful circumstances were countered by the atmosphere of the early church with its love, giving, and encouragement to the extent that the church experienced tremendous growth during this period. Indeed, God's presence and peace are most obvious when His children are supporting one another through His love. This combination of divine and human encouragement produces social support networks which afford significant stress-reduction benefits.

ARE YOU AN ENCOURAGER?

Many people believe that they are encouraging to others. Why, they can recall giving at least one encouraging remark each day. This clearly is not enough! All people—even inept ones—occasionally surprise us and do something right. We need to be ready to recognize these appropriate behaviors and comment positively upon them.

Are you an encourager now? Chances are you are not if you have to consider the question very long. But don't despair. Being an encourager is a conscious choice we all can make. When practiced regularly, encouragement becomes habitual. Encouragement is not always a possibility because some persons are unable or unwilling to accept it. Their continual refusals will eventually wear us down and we won't persist. However, this does not mean we shouldn't try initially.

Skill acquisition is paramount to successful encouragement. It is not enough to resolve to give compliments. You must develop the skills needed for effective encouragement. The remaining chapters of this book provide practical guidance in the behaviors which comprise this resource. You will learn to listen and respond effectively, to keep your compliments within realistic boundaries, to celebrate victories with others, and to supplement your encouraging words with encouraging actions. You will come to see encouragement as a motivational tool and learn to accept encouraging remarks from others. You will learn to be an encourager!

THE COST OF ENCOURAGEMENT

Encouragement is an essential ingredient in emotional and spiritual growth, but there is a cost associated with it. You see, it requires *thoughtfulness* and *consideration*. Encouragement will not naturally become a part of your behavior pattern. It will take some work.

Encouragement is not an automatic response. In fact, discouragement seems to be the response that entrenches itself without training. In Galatians 5, Paul differentiates the "works of the flesh" and the "fruit of the Spirit." Not surprisingly, numbered among the works of the flesh are hatred, discord, jealousy, fits of rage, selfish ambition, dissensions, and factions—a discouraging list of discouraging behaviors (Gal. 5:19-20). These are the *natural* responses. These are the ones with which our personalities come equipped. A little practice hones them to perfection.

In contrast to these discouraging behaviors is the fruit of the Spirit which is comprised of love, joy, peace, patience, kindness, goodness, faithfulness, gentleness, and self-control (vv. 22-23). Certainly, encouraging behaviors can be developed by nonbelievers, but what an added resource Christians have in establishing these habit patterns. You see, encouragement is really a vital component of spiritual growth. The most mature Christians should be the most encouraging ones.

Some people confuse encouragement with humanism and try to avoid both like the plague. Yet encouragement has a very sound biblical basis; it cannot be discarded merely because a secular group emphasizes its practice. Sadly, I have observed many individuals with unbiblical philosophies of life doing a better job of encouraging one another than the saints. We should be the trendsetters in this regard!

It takes *courage* to be an *encourager*. You must be courageous enough to offer praise as well as criticism. You must have the courage to thank your child for playing quietly for an hour. You must muster the courage to acknowledge your spouse's effectiveness in accounting when the checkbook balances. You must be courageous enough to commend the parishioner who can't teach Sunday School, but who always manages to show up on weekend workdays at the church. You must have the courage to change your interpersonal behaviors so that you are consistent with Scripture. If you have this courage, read on. The kingdom of God is in short supply of people who can offer the critical resource of encouragement.

3.
Getting Ready to Listen

"Ears that hear and eyes that see—the Lord has made them both" (Proverbs 20:12).

Misunderstandings—these are the stuff of which comedies are made. Yet when we are personally involved in a misunderstanding, it is not always a laughing matter.

A few years ago my wife and I bought an electric blanket with dual heating controls. Unfortunately, we failed to follow the instructions precisely and placed the controlling mechanisms on the wrong sides of the bed. Unbeknown to us, my control operated her side of the blanket and vice versa. That first night we were both miserable. I continually turned my control down because I was too hot and my wife countered by turning her control up. Now the misunderstanding seems humorous, but it certainly was no laughing matter that night.

Most misunderstandings which affect us personally have few redeeming qualities. When we wait for an hour for someone at the wrong pick-up point or when an important piece of mail is mistakenly sent to the wrong address, we are rarely amused. When we fail to hear the announcement that our eight o'clock class has been canceled or when we can't locate our children at the place we thought they told us they'd be, it is upsetting.

Misunderstandings are discouraging. The vast majority of misunderstandings arise from failure in communication and, in particular, failure to listen. If we would pay closer attention to what other people are saying to us, we could avoid many misunderstandings. This is only one of many reasons listening is an essential skill in encouragement.

Listening is perhaps the most effective element of encouraging behavior. It takes only a moment to remember how satisfied you felt when someone expressed a genuine interest in you by taking the time to listen fully to you. When others listen, you feel respected. You feel important. You feel an affinity for the listener. You are encouraged!

The fact that God listens to His children is one of the most encouraging truths in Scripture. The realization that the Almighty God delights in listening to all of His creatures is mind-boggling. However, the Bible is filled with exhortations to believers to communicate with our God. Accounts of prayers to God by all types of people in all types of circumstances abound in God's Word. These range from short utterances offered by healed lepers (Luke 17:15) to the high priestly prayer of Christ Himself (John 17). The entire Book of Psalms is a collection of praises, requests, and heartfelt expressions offered by David and others to the Lord.

We are told to approach God boldly (Heb. 4:16), casting our cares upon Him (1 Peter 5:7) and He will *listen* to us (Matt. 6:6-7). He has even provided the emphatic listening ears of His Son who can understand our every temptation, sorrow, and weakness (Heb. 4:15). This perfect listening is a vital source of spiritual encouragement.

Not surprisingly, psychologists have been quick to recognize the power of the listening ear. Schools of psychotherapy are built around the nucleus of a listening helper. Some counselors believe that listening and the communication of this act to people they are helping are the sole techniques to be used in therapy. Others supplement listening techniques with more direct action and advising. But all effective counselors spend a good deal of time learning the pivotal skill of listening to others.

Throughout my professional practice I have been reminded repeatedly of the encouraging power of the listening ear. When I was a young counselor a woman distressed about her faltering marriage came for an initial appointment. She talked for virtually the entire therapy session, pausing once in a while to allow me to say "Uh-huh" or "You must be feeling frustrated." When our time was up, I feared that she would be dissatisfied with my performance as a "silent" counselor. I was surprised to hear her say, "Oh, thank you so much for your help today. I feel so much better since you've counseled with me. You really *listened* to me. When can we meet again?"

Later, we did some important work to help her restore her marriage and involved her husband in therapy, but in that initial contact I could not have been more therapeutic. I was worried about saying too little, but I was actually most effective with my mouth virtually shut!

This example is not an isolated experience. But the benefits of listening are certainly not confined to the professional consulting room. Time and time again in my day-to-day social experiences, listening has been a very effective encouragement to others. Indeed, the listening ears of others have provided much needed encouragement for me as well.

Not surprisingly, God has acknowledged the importance of listening as an encouragement resource. Listening is the hallmark of a true friend. Conversely, the fool is characterized by his failure to listen: "He who answers before listening—that is his folly and his shame" (Prov. 18:13). God exhorts us to encourage each other through listening. Paul commands that we "carry each other's burdens, and in this way [we] will fulfill the law of Christ" (Gal. 6:2). There is no possible way to bear the burdens of another without first opening ourselves up to them through listening. God also attends us in a special way when we are open to one another. Malachi expresses it like this: "Those who feared the Lord talked with each other, and God listened and heard" (Mal. 3:16). Indeed, God's participation in the listening process of Christians automatically makes communication a three-way affair and doubles its ability to encourage.

HOW TO LISTEN

Some people have the idea that listening is an inherited characteristic. Those born without the ability to listen must make do with their limited skills. This is not the case. Listening is a skill which can be learned by anyone. It will be easier for some persons because of their personality make-up and their learning experiences. However, with proper training and practice, most people can improve their listening. Effective listeners practice their skills long hours in numerous settings. We enjoy being around people who have developed this skill because they are so encouraging and make us feel so good.

In this chapter the attitudes and skills which prepare us to listen will be explored. These are the skills which communicate our willingness to listen to others and aid in their initial sharing with us.

THE LISTENING ATTITUDE

The first step in listening is not to clean out your ears, but instead, to develop the motivation to want to hear and understand others. This is not an automatic desire. In fact, this may be the most difficult aspect of the entire task of listening. Since listening requires hard work and a lot of energy, it is easy to slack off and direct this energy elsewhere. Even though we should be open both to God and others, we often fall back into our own comfortable self-focus and forget about others.

We must respect other people before we will listen to them. Christ's personal sacrifice makes it clear that people are extremely precious to our Heavenly Father. How much less worthwhile should they be to us? James exhorts us to esteem every person with respect regardless of his station in life (James 2:1-13). This respect and genuine concern for others is the key to a listening attitude.

When we respect others, we willingly give them our time. We sincerely want to understand what they're going through. We *work* at making them feel comfortable enough with us to share with us. We are patient, especially when the other person is having difficulty expressing his true thoughts and feelings. When we respect others, we exude an encouraging attitude.

LISTENING ACTIONS

Listening is a choice we make. The most encouraging listeners are those who work diligently at mastering the requisite skills. It should be noted that the listening skills presented hereafter are devised to promote the most effective listening environment. However, some situations preclude the use of all the skills which are catalogued. If we are talking by telephone, the physical characteristics being described are irrelevant. Even in the presence of another it may be impossible in every case to drop all that we are doing and devote 100 percent attention to the person we wish to encourage. Each listening skill is important, however, and we should strive to incorporate all skills whenever possible.

How do we know when someone is really listening to us?

All of us have had the pleasurable experience of being listened to by another. Think back to one of those experiences and try to identify the actions which showed that your listener really heard you.

Psychologists have devoted a considerable amount of research to the physical behaviors that enhance and signal listening. They call these *attending* skills since they demonstrate our attendance to another. The most important attending skills include fully facing the speaker, leaning forward, maintaining eye contact, and avoiding distracting behaviors. All of these nonverbal actions *communicate* our willingness to listen to the person speaking to us. They also sharpen our observational capacities and make us aware of how congruent the speaker's words are with his actions. Remember, people are very good at camouflaging their true feelings in order to be accepted by others. "Even in laughter the heart may ache, and joy may end in grief " (Prov. 14:13). Practicing these attending skills may open your eyes to the real messages others are trying to communicate, and avert misunderstandings.

Fully Facing Others. It's amazing how often a simple skill like facing the person with whom we are conversing is not practiced. It seems so obvious that this signals our attention to others, but it is routinely ignored. I am most aware of my failures in this area when I'm around my children. My daughters, Kristen (age 6) and Anna (age 3), will not tolerate my disregard for the principle of fully facing them when we're talking. They will jump into my lap or stand directly in front of me when they wish to be heard. Even when I'm talking with someone else, my daughters remain steadfastly in front of me until they are heard. Fully facing those who talk with us is no less satisfying to adults than to our children. It is a very easy way to encourage others.

Leaning Forward. Another attending skill which is easy to practice is simply leaning toward the person to whom we are listening. Psychological researchers have discovered that the slight inclination of our bodies so that, when sitting, our forearms may rest comfortably on our thighs is an effective way to communicate care and concern for others. In the same way, leaning forward slightly when standing can be helpful and performed easily by putting one leg in front of the other.

Most of us don't think of leaning forward as a listening skill, but we practice it when we're interested in hearing another. When important things are being shared with friends, we instinctively lean toward one another. Even when an exciting sports event is on TV, we lean toward our TV screen. I notice that people often lean forward when sharing deep emotional material and that my leaning toward them can often precipitate their sharing when they are having difficulties. We often lean forward when we pray as well.

Leaning forward is an attending skill which requires balance—not the balance to prevent toppling over, but an understanding of the right amount of leaning to do. Leaning forward too far can be as detrimental to attending as leaning back. We wish to communicate caring and interest in the speaker. Leaning back may suggest that we are not really concerned about the speaker. Extreme forward leaning (besides being uncomfortable) may be interpreted as an invasion of the speaker's personal space. Monitor the effects of your leaning behavior to determine the most encouraging inclination.

Maintaining Eye Contact. The most effective nonverbal way to communicate listening and attentiveness is through eye contact. It is hard to convince a spouse or friend that we are really listening when we're reading a book or watching TV. Making eye contact with another is very encouraging. It tells the person talking to us that he is the focus of our attention. Giving our attention to him communicates that he is worthwhile and that we respect him enough to spend our time listening. This alone encourages others.

Children are especially sensitive to our eye contact. In his book, *How to Really Love Your Child* (Victor Books), Dr. Ross Campbell has detailed the crucial importance of eye contact in child-training. He describes how this action by parents helps fill their children's "emotional tanks" (their deep psychological needs). I recently saw a cartoon depicting a father reading the newspaper while his son stands alongside and complains that he needs his father's listening eyes, not just his ears. This aptly expresses the sentiments of our children so often as we ignore and discourage our most valuable resources.

Children are not subtle in their pursuit of the attention of others. They plead for our attention repeatedly with words such as, "Watch me, Daddy" or the inevitable question after they've performed something new, "Did you see me do that?" Adults are equally desirous of eye contact from others, but they usually use more tact in gaining it. Some adults gain their eye contact from others by giving it themselves. However, a good number of adults "beg" for attention by airing opinions loudly, purchasing shiny ornaments such as new cars and boats, and requesting it forthrightly with such repeated expressions as, "Look here now." I once knew a minister who must have said, "Watch this [me] carefully" twenty-five times during each of his sermons. Whether for personal gratification or assurance that his parishioners heard God's message I do not know, but he clearly needed the encouragement of "listening eyes" while he delivered his homilies. This is a need that we all share.

We communicate volumes with our eyes and encouragers should be aware of both the messages we give with our eyes and the messages given to us by the eyes of others. We must learn to "read" the eyes of others so we can know how to offer encouragement more effectively. We've all seen people who could slash through heavy brush with their glares, and others who could melt butter with the warmth of their eyes. Most of us can remember the looks of our parents which communicated pleasure or displeasure. Common expressions in our culture are communicated through eye movements such as surprise or amazement (wide-open eyes), disgust (rolling the eyes upward), and anger (squinting the eyes). Self-esteem levels are also communicated with the eyes. People with negative self-esteem spend a good deal of time looking at their shoes instead of our faces. On the other hand, giving and receiving eye contact is a good indicator of positive self-esteem.

A simple experiment which illustrates the importance of eye contact can be done by thumbing through a magazine and covering the eyes of the different people in the photographs. Make a guess about what they are experiencing. Now remove the covering from their eyes and see how much different information is given by the eyes. The mouth that seemed to be smiling is discovered to be contemplating a subject when the eyes and wrinkled forehead are uncovered. How many "eyes" made a difference in your experiment?

The amount of eye contact we should give differs with each situation. Normally, we do not have as much eye contact with strangers as we do with our good friends. In fact, the amount of eye contact between two persons is a pretty good barometer of their relationship. People who are in love look at one another much more steadily than do strangers on a train. I use this measuring stick often in marriage counseling to evaluate the closeness of the partners.

In order to maintain appropriate eye contact without shattering social customs, recognize a few unwritten rules. Speaking to another person—even saying hi to a stranger— gives you "permission" to make eye contact with him. People who are less than close friends who find themselves in close proximity to one another usually find eye contact uncomfortable. To put others at ease in this situation, keep a comfortable distance from persons not emotionally close to you before seeking eye contact. Persons with low self-esteem have difficulty maintaining eye contact. These are the folks who need a smile and your encouraging eyes the most. Don't shy away from looking at them merely because they have trouble looking back at you.

Of course, not all eye contact is encouraging. Glaring sternly into the eyes of another or staring someone down are discouraging uses of the eyes. However, maintaining positive eye contact together with a smile or look of contemplation is a very effective, encouraging behavior.

Avoid Distracting Behaviors. A final skill is a *don't* instead of a *do*. Don't engage in distracting behavior when you're trying to communicate that you're listening to another. Distracting behaviors are any nonlistening actions we perform which may command our attention or the attention of the speaker. The possibilities are endless, but here is a list of some of the more common distractions:

Rocking back and forth

Playing with your jewelry

Winding your watch

Patting your hair

Cracking your knuckles

Constantly crossing and uncrossing your legs

Simple reflection on your encounters with others will help you determine how *their* actions are distracting. Our own distracting behaviors are more difficult to discover. I well remember the first time I viewed myself counseling on videotape. It was embarassing to watch myself fiddle constantly with my ring. I had no idea that I had even touched it during the taping. In the same way your distracting actions may be unknown to you. Ask a close friend or spouse for help and they will educate you quickly. It will take some effort to eliminate these distractions, but it will be well worth it as you enhance your listening skills.

4.
You Really Heard What I Said!

"Rejoice with those who rejoice; mourn with those who mourn" (Romans 12:15).

If there was ever an individual in need of encouragement, it was Job. This Old Testament patriarch was an honest and upright man with a strong spiritual commitment. Yet in a matter of hours he lost all ten of his children in a tragic accident, his livestock and wealth, and his personal health. Three of his friends came to comfort Job and help him sort out meaning from these tragedies.

Job was obviously in both physical and emotional pain and was in dire need of encouragement. But instead of listening and offering empathic understanding, Job's friends took turns accusing him of unrighteousness and maintained that he deserved his fate.

Job hardly found these responses encouraging. He told his friends:

> I have heard many things like these; miserable comforters are you all! Will your long-winded

speeches never end? What ails you that you keep on arguing? I also could speak like you, if you were in my place; I could make fine speeches against you and shake my head at you. But my mouth would *encourage* you; comfort from my lips would bring you relief (Job 16:2-5).

Job's friends may have meant well, but their attempts at encouragement fell woefully short. Job needed some understanding words.

THE IMPORTANCE OF WORDS

Words are focal in any communication. Both the words we use and the way we use them determine how well we are received by others.

James describes the destructive potential of the tongue in his epistle, likening it to a fire which can corrupt a person and change the course of his life. Skillful orators can incite masses of people to go against their better judgment, as was evidenced by the religious leaders who urged the people of Jerusalem to ask for Jesus' death even though they had honored Him as King earlier the same week. By the same token, godly speakers often convince congregations to abandon unrighteous practices and adopt Christlike behaviors.

Even a single word can evoke a strong reaction. What happens when a preschooler repeats a profane word picked up from a playmate? Many parents go through terrible gyrations when this occurs. Such a reaction only tempts the youngster to use the word again for the attention it brings.

SHOWING WE LISTENED

Words are crucial to listening. The attending behaviors discussed in the previous chapter signal a willingness to listen and an accepting attitude. But our verbal responses prove how well we have *really* listened. In fact, for the many times that attending behaviors are impossible or impractical (telephone conversations, corresponding by mail), our words show we really have listened.

Good communicators predicate expression of personal material with a simple restatement of their partners' concerns. This lets their partners know that their opinions and feelings were respected enough to be registered before the conversation continues. This is a staple in the pool of techniques used by psychotherapists. A therapist knows that he must earn the right to offer suggestions or insights to others by listening clearly to the problems shared and evidencing that he really understands. Only when this is accomplished is permission for any additional intervention granted.

Demonstration that one has really listened is a standard communication technique taught to couples in weekend retreats and marriage counselors' offices. The skill is called "shared communication." Each spouse must listen fully to the other and restate concisely the gist of the partner's communication. Only after this can be achieved to the partner's satisfaction may other responses be given. This is by far the most effective communication skill I teach in marital counseling. It is helpful if only to inform couples (sometimes for the first time) of what the other is quarreling about.

The balance of this chapter is devoted to this communication strategy. It is a central skill in the effective encourager's repertoire and a marvelous way both to aid and endear ourselves to others.

EMPATHY

"Before you criticize me, walk a mile in my moccasins." This sentiment attributed to a wise native American represents the way we all feel when faulted unjustly. In fact, many of life's tasks *look* much easier than they are. The old story of the man and woman who traded jobs for a day illustrates this nicely. The man who argued that "women's work" was rarely taxing and demanded little exertion of energy sang quite a different song after slaving over his wife's supposedly simple tasks. We can understand completely the feelings of others only when we've experienced them ourselves. This is empathy.

The author of Hebrews cites Jesus' ability to empathize with us as a qualification for His High Priestly ministry: "For we do not have a high priest who is unable to sympathize with our weaknesses, but we have One who has been tempted in every way, just as we are—yet was without sin" (Heb. 4:15). This explanation is followed by a command that we approach the Godhead with confidence, asking for assistance in times of need since Christ completely understands our plight.

Empathy is a tall order. Empathizing is feeling *with* another person. It is entering his world and sharing his experiences. We may share excitement or distress, but we understand what he goes through. It is easiest to empathize with someone undergoing an event that we have already experienced. But sometimes we must relate to people whose lives are very different from our own. Sometimes we must empathize with someone undergoing an experience we will never have personally. Such is the case with any husband who tries to understand the feelings of his pregnant wife. And sometimes we will fail miserably at our attempts to empathize. But this doesn't excuse us from trying.

Christians have an added responsibility to be empathic: to build up the body of Christ. In writing about our spiritual gifts, Paul reminds us that each gift is to be used with love in edifying the other members of the body. The apostle then compares the body of Christ to the physical body. Since all believers are part of Christ's body, we should encourage and strengthen other believers who are undergoing difficulties and need our help. "There should be no division in the body, but that its parts should have equal concern for each other. If one part suffers, every part suffers with it; if one part is honored, every part rejoices with it" (1 Cor. 12:25-26).

Indeed, this analogy of the unity of the human body is very appropriate to our discussion of empathy. The human body reacts as a whole strongly and quickly when any of its members comes under distress. If I hit my finger with a hammer, I do not respond merely by looking at the injured finger and thinking, *That certainly hurts.* Instead, I am likely to come to the aid of that finger with all the fingers of my hand, scream loudly, and limp around as if my foot had been hurt also.

Similarly, when we feel threatened, our entire bodies respond with a generalized stress reaction. Our hearts beat faster as oxygen and sugar are sped throughout our circulatory systems to equip various muscle groups with energy to run or fight.

When the body of Christ is functioning properly, each member should seek to understand the feelings of other members. Empathic responses are those which clearly demonstrate this. In the Book of Romans, Paul tells us how to show empathy within the local church. "Rejoice with those who rejoice; mourn with those who mourn. Live in harmony with one another. Do not be proud, but be willing to associate with people of low position" (Rom. 12:15-16). Paul advises encouragers to recognize the emotional states of others and join with them in both their positive and negative emotional experiences. He also suggests that we should be willing to share in the life conditions of others to show our acceptance of them. This is perhaps a hard saying, but one that demonstrates empathy to those who are struggling.

Empathic responses often can diffuse angry situations. I once directed a counseling center which relied on an answering service to handle calls when our office was closed. One morning I picked up my messages from the preceding day and began returning them. When I identified myself to one caller, I received an angry response. She reported, "Oh! So you think there is a counseling center in our community, but I have my doubts. I called yesterday in an emergency situation expecting to deal with a professional counseling operation. Now you call a day later and ask lamely, 'May I be of assistance to you?' You really shouldn't advertise yourself as a counseling service available to this community."

Well, I had a decision on my hands here. I could clear myself of any negligence by placing the blame on my answering service which had explicit instructions to contact an available staff member in cases of emergency. This procedure was not followed and indeed the call was not labeled as urgent even the next day. This was an enticing option since it absolved me from any carelessness or unfeeling attitudes. However, it would not have helped this lady and, besides, I was responsible for the answering service I used.

Instead, I chose an empathic response. I replied, "I see that you're really disgusted. And you believe that we're unworthy of a title denoting mental health care givers."

Her voice tone was transformed dramatically and she replied, "Yes, I *was* angry." Then she began explaining the situation for which she had called the previous day and, before hanging up, thanked me for *listening* to her. An empathic response which, deep down inside, was not even the one I wanted to give had encouraged a hurting person and diffused a good deal of anger.

Empathy is best communicated through active listening. The most effective way to demonstrate that we really understand is by reflecting to the speaker the feelings and issues we have heard him communicate. Reflection is simply capsulizing the speaker's message in a brief statement. These empathic responses should rephrase the speaker's communications in the most sincere and concise manner possible.

RESPOND TO FEELING

Emotions are a very important part of our lives. Sometimes very clear and well-defined, and other times elusive, our feelings reflect who we are deep down inside and what we are going through. Positive emotions like being excited or being in love enrich our lives significantly, while disphoric emotions such as depression and anxiety disrupt our lives tremendously.

If we want really to listen to others, we cannot afford to ignore their feelings. Unfortunately, dealing with feelings is sometimes uncomfortable and seems "messy." It's easier to respond to what's going on in their worlds than how it makes them feel. Many people (particularly men) in our society seem to labor diligently at ignoring emotions. They lose touch with how they feel about things and quickly lose the ability to *feel with* others.

In marriage counseling, wives frequently complain that their husbands wouldn't recognize a feeling if one walked up and introduced itself to them. (And, of course, some wives lack the same sensitivity.) This blindness limits intimacy and shuts out one of the most exhilarating parts of being human. Emotions are God-given and should not be ignored.

Once you're willing to listen to feelings, you'll find no shortage of them in the people you wish to encourage. You need not try to "fix" the feelings of others—you can't anyway. Just acknowledge them. Responses like, "So you're feeling down," or "Sounds like you're excited," are safe. Guarded responses, at least in your initial contacts with someone, have the advantage of keeping the person from reacting defensively.

As you're listening to a person sharing his emotions, be careful to refrain from telling him how he *should* feel. There are no *shoulds* or *shouldn'ts* with feelings; they just are. You may not understand another's emotions, but don't deny or ignore them.

When reflecting emotions, be sure to use feeling words. Responses such as, "You feel like you can't get the answer" describe the situation, but do not clearly label a feeling state. It would be better to say, "You feel frustrated." Now you're not beating around the bush. In fact, using feeling words is a very direct way to encourage others. They can be communicated in one short sentence or phrase. A list of feeling words appears in Figure 1 to help you beef up your vocabulary.

A List of Feeling Words

Aggressive	Free	Misunderstood
Angry	Friendly	Nervous
Anxious	Frustrated	Pressed
Bothered	Glad	Pressured
Bored	Grateful	Powerful
Calm	Guilty	Proud
Confident	Happy	Rejected
Confused	Harassed	Relieved
Dejected	Harried	Responsible
Depressed	Hemmed in	Sad
Determined	Hostile	Scared
Disappointed	Hurt	Surprised
Down	Indecisive	Tense
Elated	Irritated	Torn
Energetic	Jittery	Trapped
Enthusiastic	Joyful	Ugly
Exhausted	Lonely	Understood
Excited	Lost	Weak

Figure 1.

It's not even necessary to possess an extensive feeling vocabulary to respond appropriately to others. You can take basic emotions like happiness, sadness, anger, or frustration and add qualifiers before them to modulate their intensity. I can say, "You're feeling a *little* angry," or "You're *very* angry," and express two different emotions. Basic emotional words are available to everyone.

Some people worry that their feeling word will be "wrong." This is rarely a serious concern. If we do label a feeling inaccurately, the person we're dealing with will usually correct us. To a person who is having trouble with a child's misbehavior, I might say, "You feel angry with Tommy." He may respond, "Really, it's not so much anger, but frustration." Even though I missed the emotion they were experiencing, I now understand them better and can encourage them more effectively.

Sometimes our feeling labels are more accurate than the person is willing to admit. To a person who has no appetite and can't sleep I may say, "You're feeling very depressed," and they may counter, "Well, maybe a little down." This gives me a cue to back down a little until the person can explore further and discover his true feelings. Then later I can use the word *depressed* and he'll likely accept it. Exploring feelings with others is sometimes like deep-sea diving—you can only go so deep so fast. Then when the other person becomes comfortable, you can go a little deeper. The effective encourager won't give up too easily.

Responding to feelings promotes further personal exploration and intimacy with the encourager. When we take the time to listen to feelings and show this by a simple statement of what we've heard, we demonstrate an enormous amount of respect to the speaker. Because this is so rarely done in our culture, we set ourselves up as special encouragers. We mirror God's concern and understanding and help others grow.

RESPONDING TO CONTENT

Usually a person expresses feelings in a context of events happening in his life. We need to acknowledge this *content* along with our feeling labels. This is readily accomplished by using some variation of the sentence, "You feel _____ *(emotion)* because _____ *(content)*."

For example, after carefully listening to a friend's disclosures about her unsatisfying prayer life, we might respond, "You feel discouraged because your prayers seem ineffective." We have acknowledged both her feeling (discouragement) and the reason she feels that way (ineffective prayers). We have demonstrated that we've heard the whole story.

Responding to content is not as taxing as labeling feelings because people are much more up front about what's going on in their worlds than about what's going on in their hearts. The primary pitfall in content reflection is long-windedness. Going on and on, repeating almost everything the speaker just said is usually a turn off. When our responses become too long, people think we're more interested in talking than listening. The more concise your response, the better.

For example, a person may report to you the following: "Things aren't going too well for me lately. My wife has had surgery twice in the last six months and my kids are getting impatient with me. I don't seem to enjoy work anymore and frankly, church has become a drag. Am I losing my salvation?"

A number of content issues are evident in this situation. Determining a common thread or general theme is most helpful. Perhaps an appropriate response would be, "You're feeling discouraged because you're not in sync with the important people and things in your life." Now the person is free to pursue any area for further exploration and sharing. You have merely shown that you were listening to the whole communication.

Be careful about questions tacked onto the end of a long disclosure. The speaker rarely is looking for an answer here. To present a comprehensive theological answer to this person's question about salvation is to miss the bulk of his struggles. Active listening is much more encouraging.

Remember to be brief. Listening demands your attention to the speaker, not eloquent speeches from you. Someone may tell you, "I've got a million things to do before the weekend. My son is coming to visit with his wife and my grandchildren and, wouldn't you know it, my husband will be out of town until Saturday afternoon. There's cleaning to do and grocery shopping. When will I ever get the time?"

An encouraging response might be, "You feel overwhelmed because you have so much to do." You must resist the urge to catalog all the tasks which face *you* this week or the desire to map out a schedule for this woman to guarantee accomplishment of all her work. Keep your response short and to the point so she'll know she's been heard.

Once you have taken the time to set up the listening environment through attending skills, and demonstrated that you really heard what your partner was trying to say by responding to both feeling and content, you may add your own perspective to the situation. But you should do this *only* after communicating listening fully. For now, your friend is encouraged enough to listen to you. In fact, it's easy to listen to someone who has taken the time to really hear what we have said.

5.
You Really Did a Good Job!

"A word aptly spoken is like apples of gold in settings of silver" *(Proverbs 25:11).*

"That was a wonderful lesson today. I haven't been challenged intellectually like that for years."

"You don't know how much it meant to the whole family for you to drop by yesterday. We are really grateful to you."

"I really appreciate your taking the kids for a walk this afternoon. It's been a tough day and they were getting on my nerves a bit. You are very thoughtful."

"The suggestion didn't work out, but thanks for trying to be helpful."

"I feel like I can talk frankly with you because you really listen."

"The methodology and results sections were very good. You need to shore up the introduction and discussion a bit and it will be an excellent article."

"You're a good daddy. I love you."

These compliments were given to me recently and it took only a few minutes of reflection to recall the warmth and encouragement generated by each one. Proverbs 25:11 states, "A word aptly spoken is like apples of gold in settings of silver." Compliments certainly fit this description. They make us feel valued and appreciated. They motivate us. They are encouraging!

Jesus was quite a complimentor. He was especially fond of recognizing the faith displayed by others. In many accounts of physical healing, Jesus publicly acknowledged the faith displayed by acquaintances. In Luke 7 Jesus is confronted by friends of a Roman soldier distressed because his servant is ill. Jesus accompanies the messengers toward the centurion's home and is met by persons who relay a message from the centurion. He requests that Jesus merely speak the word to heal the servant rather than come all the way to his home. To this demonstration of faith, Jesus paid special tribute. "When Jesus heard this, He was amazed at him, and turning to the crowd following Him, He said, 'I tell you, I have not found such great faith even in Israel'" (Luke 7:9). Christ recognized the faith of this foreigner and commended him to those in attendance. Similar pronouncements were given to the woman healed of a blood disease who merely touched Him in a crowd (Mark 5:34), the paralytic lowered through the roof of a house to be healed (Luke 5:24), and the prostitute who repentantly washed His feet with her tears (Luke 7:50).

Jesus was fair in His commendations of others. He minced no words condemning the scribes and Pharisees for their internal unrighteousness, but He also complimented a Pharisee who responded accurately in a conversation (Mark 12:34). He complimented the faith of the chief tax collector, Zaccheus (Luke 19:8-9), and identified faith deficits when His disciples displayed them.

Honest communications are usually very encouraging, especially when expressed tactfully. In this chapter we shall explore the use of compliments, praise, and realistic feedback.

WHAT TO COMPLIMENT

Let's say we want to make an encouraging remark to Sheila. Where do we start? Well, she is wearing a pretty dress. Why not start there? Or we could compliment the way she answered the objections raised at the business meeting. Then there's her children. We really do think they are darling. And let's not forget her vocal solo last Sunday.

If given sincerely, compliments in any of these areas will probably be encouraging. Researchers have found that we are most likely to compliment the performance of others or their appearance.[5] However, the most valued and meaningful compliments are those few which tell us something nice about our personality. Encouraging remarks about who we are as individuals are very gratifying because they reassure us that we're OK because of *who* we are, not *what* we do. Unfortunately, these are the rarest type of compliments given in our society.

Of course, this does not mean that we should abandon other compliments. But there is even a pecking order among these. It is better to compliment people for things they do rather than for their appearance. Appearance is modifiable only up to certain limits and we really can't escape the effects of time and heredity. Compliments such as, "You look good" are destined to be followed up with "For someone your age" at some point in time.

We have much better control over our performance than our looks. It is usually encouraging to have our work recognized. This is especially true when we have put a good deal of effort into a task. In fact, acknowledgment of our effort may be more encouraging than simply complimenting the results. This is the sentiment expressed in the maxim: It's not whether you win or lose, but how you play the game.

Unfortunately, many offer praise according to another standard: Winning isn't everything. It's the *only* thing. Complimenting sincere effort falls more in line with biblical teaching since imperfection is recognized as the norm among humans. Thank goodness God allows for errors in that long process called the Christian life. It's alright to say, "You're really coming along in that word study class. I can see a lot of improvement."

We need to become good at catching people doing things right. Most of us need little help in learning to identify peoples' faults. But when someone is acting responsibly, we should use this occasion to encourage them instead of ignoring the event. In one of the most encouraging letters in the New Testament, the Apostle Paul demonstrates this principle in his own discussion of encouragement. As was Paul's practice, he ended his first letter to the Thessalonians with some instructions for practical Christian living. He exhorted them to "encourage one another and build one another up" (1 Thes. 5:11). And in the same verse he recognized that these believers were already doing a good job in this area, so he added, "Just as in fact you are doing." Often, it is easy to give directives but difficult to recognize when someone is already following them. A directive can often be transformed from a discouragement into an encouragement when we recognize the success that someone has already achieved in that area.

WHEN COMPLIMENTS AREN'T ENCOURAGING

Of course, not all compliments are encouraging. Anytime we believe that a compliment is laced with an ulterior motive, it is viewed with contempt. Using compliments manipulatively or "buttering up" someone is inappropriate as it demonstrates disregard and disrespect for the person. This is a form of selfishness, a violation of the biblical directives requiring openness and honesty in our communications with one another.

Compliments are also unwelcomed for other reasons. We usually do not appreciate compliments from individuals who strike us as having poor taste or being unintelligent. We see their praise as an indictment of undesirability instead of an encouragement.

A real problem in our culture is that insincere compliments are given so frequently that it sometimes becomes difficult to believe others when they say something good about us. With some people, compliments are a dime a dozen. They hand them out with the frequency that a politician shakes hands: "Oh! That's simply a beautiful dress." "I just love your new hairstyle." The recommendation letter is a case in point. Most letters of recommendation are highly complimentary and exceed realistic assessments of the person being recommended. Many times employers will red flag a recommendation letter that is even neutral because this is so divergent from the norm. They reason that the person must have faults so glaring that the reference writer could not ignore them.

The old adage: "Say something nice or don't say anything at all" is really not the best advice. It should be amended to read: "Say something sincerely or don't say anything at all." Our phoniness is detected far more readily than most of us realize. It renders our attempts at encouragement useless.

It is also imperative that we acknowledge the emotions of the person we are complimenting. Failure to acknowledge another's feelings often renders statements meant to be encouraging, discouraging. I well remember the discouragement I felt from some well-intentioned compliments received from one of my dearest friends during my graduate studies. After completing all of my graduate course work, I was required to take comprehensive examinations over the entire field of counseling psychology. These exams entailed three full eight-hour days of writing, and were dreaded intensely by every doctoral student in our department. The exams were offered only twice per year and one was allowed to take the exams only twice. Failure to complete these tests successfully in two tries meant automatic expulsion from the doctoral program and three years of coursework down the drain. With thus much of my life riding on my performance on these tests, you can understand some of my apprehension and self-doubts in anticipating this evaluation.

My major professor was one of my strongest supporters during those graduate years and remains a dear friend and colleague to this day. However, just before the week of testing he inquired about my emotional status. I reported that I was anxious about the upcoming comprehensive examinations. To this he replied, "David, we're not concerned about you at all. I know you will perform exceptionally on the tests."

These words were meant to be reassuring and encouraging, but they were neither. Ken had failed to acknowledge my feelings of anxiety and understand why I might feel anxious. Therefore, his reassurances were not very reassuring. In fact, his comments induced even more stress. You see, besides all my other fears associated with the possibility of failing the examinations, I also feared that I would disappoint my professor. His stated faith in my abilities was interpreted as a perfectionistic demand upon me which was threatening.

It would have been much more reassuring for him to say, "I know you're anxious right now and that's only natural. But I have confidence that you'll overcome the anxiety and perform well like you usually do." In this response, my feelings are acknowledged and confidence is instilled based upon an objective standard (my past academic performance). Failure to recognize emotions and handing out blind reassurances to others can be very discouraging.

BE REALISTIC

Sometimes the most encouraging comments we receive are not flowery compliments at all, but rather honest feedback about ourselves. It is refreshing to hear realistic assessments of our performance from those who really care about us. As Proverbs 28:23 advises, "He who rebukes a man will in the end gain more favor than he who has a flattering tongue."

Realistic feedback is often sorely needed since we usually have difficulty seeing ourselves objectively. This is even true of our physical appearance. Have you ever shuddered after seeing yourself in a picture shot by an unannounced photographer, or winced when you looked up suddenly into an unsuspected mirror? These "unbecoming" images we see may be more indicative of our normal appearance than we think. Most persons automatically pose in front of a mirror or for a photographer, instinctively tilting their heads in the most favorable position without awareness of these movements. There's a good chance that we also modify other characteristics about ourselves to meet our personal expectations. We need the observations of others to give us an accurate perspective.

Failure to receive realistic feedback from others can have some very unfortunate consequences. Surrounding ourselves with "yes-men" rarely contributes to personal growth and achievement. Celebrities often bemoan the fact that their closest associates are nonhelpful because of reluctance to render sincere evaluations. This is reminiscent of the monarch in the fairy tale "The Emperor's New Clothes." He paraded unclad before his subjects who, except for a young child, were afraid to admit aloud that their ruler had been duped by a crafty tailor into believing that an imaginary set of fine clothing was visible to all but himself.

Noncritical associates can be a scourge to modern-day leaders as well. Historians documenting President John F.

Kennedy's administration often contrast the disastrous Bay of Pigs invasion with his successful handling of the Cuban missile crisis. During the discussion surrounding the Bay of Pigs invasion of Cuba, Kennedy's aides and cabinet members were reluctant to express any objections to the military plan presented to them. Any dissension was squelched by the group; thus, the realistic appraisal of the glaring flaws in the plan were not realized until the blunder was underway. Learning from that experience, President Kennedy welcomed dissent from his associates during deliberations on methods to handle the Russians' shipments of nuclear arms to Cuba and he was rewarded by a much more encouraging outcome when he acted.

We all desperately need honest evaluations from others—relating to both our positive and negative strivings. These encouragements may even hurt initially, but reap long-term rewards.

A good deal of my energy as a professional psychotherapist is devoted to listening to persons sharing their struggles and to giving them my honest impressions of their contributions to their suffering as well as strategies for overcoming difficulties. Realistic feedback is imperative. Anything less may hamper their ability to understand their circumstances and personality variables, and may deny them the insights needed to produce change. Anything less may be quite discouraging.

I well remember working with Harry, a young graduate student who was struggling with mild depression. Harry was losing interest in his job, his social life, and his studies. He was very bright, but on the verge of flunking out of graduate school because of his low mood state. Week after week in therapy we discussed his concerns and soon I found myself losing energy in my sessions with Harry. His depression was taking a toll on me as I tried to enter his world and understand his feelings. Soon I felt a responsibility to share my feelings with Harry. I disclosed to him how my energy was being drained somewhat in our counseling sessions and hypothesized that this may be happening in many of his social relationships. Harry took inventory of his interpersonal relationships during the next week and found that many friends were beginning to withdraw from him because he was wearing them down. He quickly took steps to modify his behavior toward others and actually recovered from his depression shortly afterward. Upon termination we discussed his progress in therapy and Harry reported that my honest feedback had been the turning point in his emotional struggles. He said, "I never knew how I was affecting others until you told me. I thought I was getting depressed because others were withdrawing. I never dreamed I was driving them away. Telling me the truth was the most important thing you did for me."

HOW TO GIVE REALISTIC FEEDBACK

Clearly, some precautions are in order when seeking to encourage others through providing realistic feedback. When assessments are given without the benefit of a supportive relationship, they are rarely encouraging. Instead, they are interpreted as unwanted intrusions, unsolicited advice, or unfriendly criticisms. Being informed that you have bad breath may be welcomed from a concerned spouse, but seen as a put-down from a new acquaintance. Likewise, being told that you lifted your head on a stroke by a golfing buddy may be interpreted as a helpful hint; but when given the same information by a person on a nearby tee, it feels intrusive and critical. If you fear that your observations may not be wanted, simply ask if the person desires your input.

Encouraging feedback demands honesty. Anything less may placate someone for a short while but will usually be recognized as a lie in the long run. We hold people who lie to us in contempt when their falsehoods are discovered, especially if their untruthfulness causes us embarrassment or contributes to their personal gain. As Proverbs 29:5 warns, "Whoever flatters his neighbor is spreading a net for his feet." It is socially dangerous to emulate Professor Harold Hill, the unscrupulous salesman in "The Music Man" who convinced the good citizens of River City that their children were natural instrumentalists so he could pocket some fast cash. Flattery that gives inaccurate information to others and raises false hopes is cruel as well as discouraging.

Give feedback only in areas in which you are knowledgeable. Everyone is entitled to his personal tastes; often sharing your perspective on a matter is helpful. Reassuring a friend that his new suit is properly tailored or encouraging another to try out a well-conceived plan may be quite appropriate. However, offering feedback in areas where we possess only modest expertise is rarely encouraging or helpful. It is irritating to hear a childless adult evaluate the child-rearing practices of a parent, or to receive a critique of your medical regimen by a person who wouldn't know the difference between an aspirin and an antibiotic. If you cannot offer helpful feedback, offer none at all.

When possible, offer *corrective* feedback—that is, do not stop at merely describing a problem you see, but offer a possible solution for consideration. The ideas and behaviors of others may not seem so dysfunctional when we try to identify an alternate way to approach their concern. It's easy to say, "I wouldn't do that." It's much more difficult to offer another reasonable option. However, if you can build a better mousetrap, others will usually want to see your plan.

Offering corrective feedback is best accomplished when we are very specific in our observations. Telling a friend that others have trouble listening to her is not as helpful as saying, "I've noticed that people begin looking away and seem uncomfortable when you complain about your job.

However, everyone seems quite interested in the other topics you discuss."

I became acutely aware of the importance of useful feedback when submitting articles to professional journals for publication. The editor makes a decision to accept, reject, or ask for a revision of an article based on the blind reviews of other professionals in the field. Accepting a manuscript for publication is the feedback the author wants to hear. However, when the article is rejected or a revision is requested, very specific reasons and guidelines help enormously. Reviewers who tell you simply to revise the introduction succeed only in inducing perplexity. Those who advise you to emphasize or enlarge a particular part of the introduction and cut paragraph three have given you corrective feedback.

When I became a manuscript reviewer, I discovered that the process of giving authors corrective feedback was not an easy task. I may not like the way paragraph eight sounds, but I must go beyond my personal tastes and identify the problem for the author or accept her ideas and wording. Only then am I doing the author a service.

In summary, the ability to provide realistic feedback to others can be an effective tool in the encourager's repertoire. However, our output becomes discouraging and irritating if we fail to observe several guidelines for its use. Feedback is only welcomed if we have a supportive relationship with another. We must be honest in our communications even if it hurts. Also, it is essential that we offer observations only in those areas in which we are knowledgeable. Corrective feedback that is specific and supplemented with ideas for improvement is the most encouraging.

6.
*You Think **I** Could Do That?*

"But commission Joshua, and encourage and strengthen him, for he will lead this people across and will cause them to inherit the land that you will see" (Deuteronomy 3:28).

In the sports arena, encouragement is a potent tool. Athletes often credit their fans' support for their superior accomplishments, reporting that they received additional energy and increased their skill levels when "the fans got behind us." Sportswriters and announcers speak of the "home court advantage."

By the same token, encouragement provides the motivation to excel in many life tasks. People can function only to the degree that they feel adequate to function. Therefore, increasing a person's belief that he can achieve a goal is an essential part of encouraging him. This is real motivation.

We all need motivation to enjoy life fully. We need a good deal of motivation to maintain our spiritual lives as well. Motivated Christians are more inclined to do the things they realize they should do. They are more open to "spiritual stretching"—branching out in new areas. They also approach life with an exciting fervor which is contagious to those around them. What a powerful and encouraging witness!

USING GUILT TO MOTIVATE

Not all motivation stems from encouragement. In fact, encouragement is hardly the favored mode to dispense this critical energy. Most of use would rather use guilt. Of course, not all guilt is without merit. Feeling the pangs of conscience and the internal tug of the Holy Spirit when we commit or contemplate sin is a necessary motivating force to produce corrective action. But most of the guilt we experience hardly has spiritual roots or connotations.

Guilt is frequently used as the leverage to motivate us to do things that we would not naturally choose. Parents use it. Pastors use it. Advertisers use it to coerce us into all sorts of commitments we would rather not make. We buy expensive encyclopedias for six-month-old Johnny because the salesperson convinces us that we'll retard the baby's intellectual growth if we spend our money elsewhere. Guilt used in this way is merely manipulation.

Guilt may motivate us to do some things, but it does not evoke a smiling face or a cheerful attitude. It is hardly encouraging.

EFFECTIVE MOTIVATION

Psychologist Robert White offers an alternative to guilt which he calls "effectance motivation."[6] Effectance motivation springs from our inherent need to explore and interact with our environment. It is pleasurable and intrinsically rewarding. Effectance motivation relies upon encouragement to promote new activities and give permission to be imperfect.

Effectance motivation differs from guilt-induced motivation in several ways. Effectance motivation uses a person's natural tendency to learn about and master his environment, while guilt creates a specific deficit which must be filled. Effectance motivation allows for numerous and novel approaches to a situation, while guilt usually circumscribes a single response to a situation. Effectance motivation is rewarding. It makes us feel good about what we're doing and we want to do it again. Guilt may procure the desired response, but often it is a begrudging one. When we do something because someone makes us feel guilty, we are very likely to quit the action when this person goes away. It may not have long-lasting effects. Effectance motivation makes us feel one-up while guilt makes us feel one-down.

Churches often sponsor programs to meet the physical and spiritual needs of the underprivileged. To fund these programs, a minister may use guilt-induced motivation. He may chide parishioners for being affluent in the first place and berate them for expenditures on luxuries while others go wanting for necessities. He may make the people feel bad enough so they'll give money to soothe a guilty conscience.

The same minister could use effectance motivation to accomplish this goal. In this case he will describe very clearly the needs of the deprived. However, instead of berating his parishioners for their selfishness and insensitivity, he can arrange for some of his audience to visit the needy firsthand. This may motivate some of the churchgoers to give of themselves to the underprivileged in addition to giving their money.

SELF-EXPECTATIONS

It is often said that you get what you look for. This applies not only to what we look for in others but also what we expect of ourselves as well. After teaching a person a new

69

skill, I always listen intently for his prediction of how the new behavior will work for him. Persons who expect successful implementation of the skill in their lives usually profit greatly. Those who predict failure are clearly telling me we've got more work to do before we can expect improvement. Their expectations of failure are rarely disappointed.

Self-expectations not only predict future performance, but they also actually determine it. If we enter a social gathering expecting to be ignored, we'll position ourselves in inconspicuous places and be overlooked. If we go to bed expecting to have difficulty falling asleep, we're in for a lot of tossing and tumbling. If we expect to deliver a speech with humor and gusto, we'd better prepare for an appreciative audience.

Researchers have found that self-expectations significantly affect the *aggressiveness* with which we attack a task, the *persistence* which we evidence in the pursuit, and the *degree of optimism* which we entertain.[7] In other words, self-expectations of success motivate us to try harder, try longer, and anticipate positive results. Self-expectations of failure cannot sustain enough personal motivation for success because we only try halfheartedly and we give up at the first obstacle encountered. It's easy to see how a person with low expectations of himself garners a lot of evidence to prove his case. Motivation to change his outlook will almost assuredly have to come from the encouragement of others.

TAKING RISKS

To learn a new response, we first must take the initiative to try out the behavior and then practice it. This seems obvious since we know that we can't become good at something without first doing it. Encouragement frequently can provide the necessary push to get us to begin something new.

Often learning to do new things requires personal risk-taking. This can be uncomfortable and keep us from trying new things. For instance, a young man may wish desperately to develop a romantic relationship with a young lady, but may fear asking her for a date. Or a man may be a very knowledgeable student of the Bible but fear taking the risk to stand up in front of a Sunday School class to share his insights.

Verbal persuasions, when given within realistic boundaries, motivate us as they encourage us to take some initial risks. In Matthew 14 we see an example of encouragement being used by Jesus to motivate Peter to take a risk. The disciples were out on a boat in the middle of the night in stormy weather. Jesus came to them walking on the water and, as a group, they were terrified. They believed they were seeing a ghost. Jesus identified Himself and tried to encourage His associates: "Take courage! It is I. Don't be afraid" (Matt. 14:27).

Then Peter asked Jesus if he too could walk on the water. The Lord encouraged him and Peter took a risk stepping out of the boat. Indeed, he walked upon the water for a short time before he took his eyes off Jesus and started to sink. And even though Peter showed only a little faith, he showed a lot more faith than his eleven companions. Jesus' words encouraged him to take a big risk. When Peter began to sink, Jesus responded honestly by identifying his lack of faith. Jesus' encouragement motivated Peter during this incident and afterward to take many risks for the kingdom of God.

God's encouragement frequently motivated the nation of Israel to engage in risk-taking behaviors. In Deuteronomy 31 Moses turned over the national leadership to Joshua. He charged all the people to capture the land promised by saying, "Be strong and courageous. Do not be afraid or terrified because of [the Canaanites], for the Lord your God goes with you; He will never leave you nor forsake you" (v. 6).

Later, when the Israelites were engaged in a civil war

occasioned by the misbehavior of the Benjamites, the Israelites encouraged one another to regroup and fight again after
suffering 22,000 casualties on the battlefield the day before.
This mutual encouragement provided a very strong motivation for extreme risk-taking behavior (Judges 20).

God even used Israel's enemies to encourage His people in
battle. In Judges 7, Gideon exercised tremendous faith in
selecting only 300 men to fight a large army of Midianites.
God recognized the understandable apprehension that Gideon and his men experienced the night before the battle and
sought to motivate Gideon in verses 10 and 11: "If you are
afraid to attack, go down to the camp with your servant
Purah and listen to what they are saying. Afterward, you will
be *encouraged* to attack the camp." On the spy mission,
Gideon discovered that the Midianites were ripe for defeat.
This encouragement motivated Gideon to lead his army to
victory that very evening.

A good way to reduce the threat associated with a new
behavior is to change the way we think about the risks. This
involves reframing a new situation as a challenge instead of a
threat. This is precisely the strategy the Apostle Paul used in
all of his missionary endeavors. Whether being welcomed to
a friendly church or imprisoned by Roman soldiers, he
looked upon every experience as a challenge to evangelize
and teach those around him (Phil. 4:11).

When we reframe a threat as a challenge, it inspires
creativity. Meeting a challenge is a positive goal which
ngenders self-expectations of success. It motivates us to
keep plugging away when problems are encountered. It gen-
erates effectance motivation.

PERSISTENCE

Accomplishing most significant endeavors requires a good
deal of persistence. Persistence is the gauge of motivation;

frequently it is the point of breakdown in a thwarted task. We fail to remain persistent and give up too soon.

Researchers have shown that persistence is affected by our history of success at similar tasks, the frustration levels we encounter, and the way rewards are meted out.[8] Naturally, we are more persistent when we've succeeded at the task before. We are also most persistent when we encounter a mild degree of frustration. Excessive frustration levels are discouraging, but the complete absence of frustration makes a task boring. A mild degree of frustration (a degree that we can overcome) creates a challenge. Also it's most advantageous to receive a reward immediately after we earn it, as this keeps us pressing on to the end.

Suppose your car needs new spark plugs and you decide to change them yourself. If you've ever changed the spark plugs before [past success], you'll feel more confident, expect success, and probably persist even when you need more strength to remove the spark plug wires than ever before. Then there's the actual removal of the spark plugs themselves. You are much more likely to persist if your efforts result in small advances every few minutes [minimal frustration] than if you convince yourself, after giving it your best effort, that someone welded the spark plugs into the engine one night while you were sleeping. You will persist longer as well if you happen to need the car that afternoon [immediate reinforcement]. If this is the case, we trust your optimal frustration level will not be exceeded.

HOW TO MOTIVATE OTHERS THROUGH ENCOURAGEMENT

Motivating others is a big business in our country. Salespersons often meet daily to encourage each other mutually. Politicians rally their supporters around themselves to deliver pep talks for renewed vigor in campaigning. Professors present compelling arguments to their students to justify the importance of their courses (and the $75 price tag of the required texts).

The fact is that people have a tremendous impact on the motivation of other people. We influence others by our words and even by our subtle eye movements. Strangers have the ability to increase or quell motivation by offering encouraging or discouraging judgments of our behaviors. Good encouragers are effective motivators.

The Attitudes That Motivate Others. It's refreshing to be around someone with a winning attitude. We choose these people to run our businesses, coach our athletic teams, and govern us. In Christian ministry they are the most effective soul-winners, ministers, and teachers. People with a winning attitude motivate others. The coach with a winning attitude may not be able to dunk the basketball or tackle the fullback, but his optimistic outlook and love for the game have been infused into his players.

What are the components of this motivating attitude? A major one is optimism—not a blind faith that everything will work out magically in the end, but a realistic appraisal of the facts and a belief that improvement can come with time and proper training. Persons with motivating attitudes are not immobilized by failure. They recognized failure as a necessary aspect of learning and accept others when the chips are down. They keep in mind the big picture.

Effective motivators make little use of guilt. Instead, they ally the intrinsic motivation we already have to deal successfully with challenging tasks. Effective motivators know that guilt impairs our motivation and reduces our ability to enjoy an accomplishment. A guilt-motivated success is merely an escape from a negative outcome, not a positive experience in and of itself.

The Words That Motivate Others. Ours is a culture which enjoys hearing the encouraging words of others. Whether to hear an evangelist motivate us to new spiritual heights or to hear a promoter motivate us to sell more soap, Americans come in droves, pack large auditoriums, and even pay money to be motivated by others. We like to hear others tell us what we can accomplish.

Exactly what are these motivating words? Some of the most motivating words are those which express positive expectations of others. It's amazing how often we neglect to tell others that we have confidence in them. We're much better at saying, "I knew you could do it" *after* an accomplishment than predicting the success beforehand. This is tragic since verbalized positive expectations are so integral to motivation. In marriage counseling it is not uncommon to hear a husband say, "I knew she could do it all the time," as the wife chimes in quickly, "Well, why didn't you tell me *before* I started?" Or worse yet, the wife might reply, "That's the first time I've ever heard you say that."

Other motivating words are those which encourage us to take the risks necessary to try something new. It's amazing how often we shy away from things we'd really like to do because we overestimate the consequences of failure. When a new opportunity arises, I regularly observe people begging their friends with their eyes to tell them to try it. People often need that little push, that simple permission to attempt a new task. The real need, of course, is to be assured that they will be accepted even if they fail.

Recently when leaving a church service in which individuals from the congregation had shared songs, prayers, and testimonies, I overheard a man say to his wife, "I never said you couldn't stand up." She replied, "But you never said I could either." This husband had squandered a perfect opportunity to motivate his wife with very minimal effort—a move that may have blessed many parishioners and strengthened his marital relationship. Be willing to say aloud, "Go ahead and try it" and let your partner know you'll be there regardless of the outcome.

Motivating words are not limited to mere positive pronouncements. Offering correction is often a very motivating communication. Constant failure experiences sap our motivation significantly. When we help others see how they might overcome an obstacle, it breathes new life into their incentive. This is the reason many people seek help through psychotherapy. I have often profited in renewed motivation from the timely advice and correction of others. Whether from careful instruction on how to correct a slice that plagued my golf game or a small (but critical) piece of information which helped me master a calculation for my tax form, corrective feedback has put me on the right track and rejuvenated energy to enjoy or at least complete a previously frustrating task. A word of caution is in order here. Corrective feedback is appreciated only when its receiver has given you permission (stated or implied) to share it. Be careful to refrain from being the "answer man."

Actions That Motivate Others. We always place more confidence in the words of others when they practice what they preach. Indeed, demonstrating our faith in others and taking a risk that we are persuading them to take can be very motivating. Modeling is particularly helpful because it shows others what they can expect if they attempt the same task. Your actions also give them a game plan to follow (or avoid, if you fail).

Engineer success experiences for others whenever possible. Since success breeds more success, help others do well when they attempt a new task. I often try to insure an early diet of success when a person I'm working with learns a new skill by assigning homework for its use in a setting that will maximize the possibility of rewarding him. He should practice his new assertive skills with a family member requesting small favors before tackling a request for a substantial raise from his boss. This seems rather commonsensical, but the principle is routinely violated. We motivate others to try something new and then give them insurmountable tasks. These early failure experiences are discouraging and drain us of motivation. Sometimes we never attempt the task again. This doesn't imply that we have to make things easier for others any time we encourage them to take a risk. This is impossible as many things exceed our control. But a little careful planning can be very effective.

There are a few cautions which should be observed when contemplating motivating actions. Do not turn play into work by giving external rewards for things that people do for their own enjoyment. Behavioral psychologists have shown that they can discourage children from playing with a toy that was once enjoyed greatly merely by giving them an external reward (e.g. candy) for playing with the toy. After children have been paid to play with the toy, they aren't interested in playing with it for free at a later time. Money has the uncanny ability to transform play into work and sap motivation from the task. Also be realistic when persuading others to take risks. If John can barely negotiate chewing bubble gum and walking at the same time, don't try to convince him that he's the logical choice for quarterback on the school football team. Remember that a small level of frustration may actually encourage persistence, but large levels are very discouraging.

7.
Encouraging Actions

"Well done, good and faithful servant! You have been faithful with a few things; I will put you in charge of many things" (Matthew 25:21).

A few years ago a wealthy New York executive made headlines when he was invited back to his childhood junior high school to deliver a commencement address. He had prepared a glowing speech to encourage and challenge the students to continue their education and realize their potential in the world. However, when he arose to deliver his prepared remarks, he saw the faces of his audience—poor children in a school system which had a better than 50 percent drop-out rate. Recognizing that his words alone, albeit encouraging ones, would have little effect on the fate of these children, he dispensed with his notes in favor of encouraging actions. He promised every graduating student a college education at his own expense if they completed high school and met college admission standards. Moreover, he maintained personal contact with his "investments" to encourage them. A college education was out of the reach of most of these poor inner-city children; thus, they had little incentive to work diligently in high school. Now they had a chance at the same opportunities as their middle- and upperclass counterparts. Not surprisingly, the retention rate of this class greatly surpasses that of other New York students with similar socio-economic characteristics. All this because someone was willing to "put his money where his mouth was." He took the challenge to *act* encouragingly.

The New Testament Epistle of James is one of the most practical books in the Bible. This early pastor of the church in Jerusalem was very concerned about the outworking in day-to-day life of one's faith. In chapter 2, verse 20 James renders those often quoted words, "Faith without works is dead" (KJV).

We can say the same thing about encouragement. If we tell someone that she has valuable insights and would be an able discussion group leader, but never ask her to take on this task, she will soon question the sincerity of our (supposedly) encouraging remark. We must be willing to back up our encouragement with actions which demonstrate that we have been truthful in our appraisals of another's capabilities. Encouragement without accompanying actions is dead.

To make use of some popular sayings, "Talk is cheap" and "Actions speak louder than words." A parent who tells her teenager that he is a good and courteous driver is most convincing when she gives him the car keys. A husband who says he's supportive of his wife's new job outside the home is most believable when he is clearing the table after supper or giving the children baths. Encouraging actions give our encouraging words credibility.

SHOWING CONFIDENCE

Perhaps the most encouraging actions are those which demonstrate confidence in our abilities. When we tell someone that we believe in them, we'd better be ready to show it. This does not routinely happen. When owners of professional sports teams publicly reiterate their faith in a beleaguered coach through a "vote of confidence," the headlines of newspapers read "Coach on His Way Out." Unfortunately, the same is often true in government, schools, business, and even Christian organizations.

Showing confidence is not a difficult task. It merely means that we back up what we say aloud with what we do. If I say I believe someone, I don't look for corroborating witnesses. If I encourage someone to enter a worthwhile ministry, I should be willing to contribute to it.

We can best show confidence in others by first giving them both the permission and the opportunity to act on their own, and then refraining from offering constant advice and making inspections of their every move. I hardly feel confident when you tell me my gardening is excellent, but keep suggesting different ways to tend the plants or follow behind me redoing my work. This is a common complaint I hear from college students in the counseling office. The students are frustrated because their parents, who insist that they have complete confidence in their collegian's judgment and readiness to make everyday decisions, call constantly to remind them of everything from the amount of detergent to use in the wash to the relative importance of grades over social activities. These parents' demonstrated lack of confidence in their children is very discouraging and almost always has undesirable effects. Most students become angry at the insincerity these calls evidence and sometimes do just the opposite of what is advised. Some, however, come to depend on their parents' directives and fail to develop the confidence in their own decision-making abilities that the college environment is ideally suited to foster. Inevitably the parents later wonder why their child has failed to grow up and individuate from the family.

This discouraging behavior is not limited to parents. Anytime we "check up" on someone in whom we've reported we have confidence, we invalidate our claim. I well remember the historic day in my marriage when I turned the financial bookkeeping over to my wife. I took considerable pride in my management abilities even though overseeing the assets and expenditures of a poor graduate student hardly qualified me as a skilled accountant. I told Nan how much faith I had in her financial management skills and how confident I was of continued checkbook accuracy. I ceremonially bequeathed the records to her. Then I proceeded to check and doublecheck her performance and decisions, effectively nullifying all my stated confidence. Never mind that her degree in business significantly outranked my psychology degree in the money-management field; I maintained a watchful eye on the record-keeping until it became painfully evident that she could outperform me at the task. (And as the bank statement arrives monthly I thank God for her proficiency.)

My behavior was exactly wrong! I talked a very encouraging talk, but my actions were anything but encouraging. Nan had every right to challenge my stated vote of confidence and order me out of the books. Fortunately, she never doubted her ability to manage the resources admirably and (fortunately for me) she is quite long-suffering. However, for many our discouraging actions invalidate our stated encouragement and contribute to feelings of personal inadequacy.

WHEN SOMEONE FAILS

Backing encouraging words with encouraging actions is especially appropriate when someone has failed. Of course, it is helpful to reassure someone verbally; however, when we act on our encouragement, it is doubly helpful. Jesus aptly demonstrated this principle in His relationship with His disciple, Peter. Simon Peter was a man who was anything but noncommittal. During the Last Supper he adamantly swore allegiance to Jesus Christ, claiming that he would never forsake his Master. Jesus promptly predicted that Peter would deny Him three times that very night. Just as predicted, Peter disclaimed association with Jesus on three difference occasions the night of Christ's arrest. He became very discouraged about his failure to maintain his commitment to his Master, and the Scriptures say that he went out and wept bitterly.

After Christ's resurrection He appeared to Peter and some of the other disciples on the shores of the Sea of Galilee. Jesus questioned Peter directly asking, "Do you truly love Me?" To this Peter replied, "Yes, Lord, You know that I love You," using a less intense word for *love* than Jesus used in His question, in light of Peter's recent denials. Jesus then told Peter to feed His sheep. A second time Jesus asked Peter about his love for Him and a second time Peter responded similarly, using the less intense word for love. Jesus again instructed Peter to take care of His sheep. Then the third time, to match Peter's three denials, Jesus asked Peter if he really loved Him. This time Jesus used the less intense word for *love* and Peter replied accordingly. Then Jesus once again told Peter to feed His sheep (John 21:15-17).

In this touching narrative Jesus gave Peter an opportunity to demonstrate his commitment even though he had failed miserably at this only days before. But Jesus did not stop merely with a request for lip service about commitment from Peter. Instead, He entrusted Peter with a very important ministry in the Lord's service. Jesus reassured Peter of his importance to an ongoing Christian work by assigning him a prominent ministry—even though he had experienced failure. Christ went further still and predicted a long ministry for His disciple. This assignment was clearly an encouragement to Peter, who devoted the entirety of his life to carrying out the instructions to feed Christ's sheep.

We would do well to follow Christ's example of encouraging someone who has failed. Instead, we often take the "one strike and you're out" stance. Oh yes, we'll still talk to the person, but heaven knows he never deserves another *real* opportunity to try again. In therapy I often meet with discouraged men and women who bemoan the fact that they can never regain their parents' trust because of a failure decades earlier. The same is true in Christian service. Christians are often guilty of shooting their wounded. In most modern churches Peter would never have received another chance to feed Christ's sheep. We must willingly supplement our encouraging talk with actions which show that we give second chances.

ENCOURAGING ACTIONS SHOULD BE REALISTIC

If our actions are to be confidence boosters, they must be realistic. Giving people responsibilities which overtax their skills is quite discouraging. Assigning a suicidal patient to a beginning counselor is not the way to break the counselor in. Elevating a new convert to the position of deacon or elder is no way to enhance spiritual growth. Encouraging actions should be commensurate with a person's abilities.

Responsibilities must be tailored to the individual. Though all persons are created equal in terms of worth, there are glaring inequalities in just about every other dimension. Some people are more intelligent than others. Some are more mechanically inclined. Some are more socially adept. The same opportunity may be quite encouraging when given to one, and just the opposite to another.

In Matthew 25, Jesus gives a series of parables emphasizing the importance of watching for His second coming. In one parable, a master preparing to go on a long journey entrusts his property to his servants. Apparently, he was a good judge of the business acuity of his servants and entrusted them with differing amounts of money. To one, he gave five talents (a large sum of money); to another, two talents; and to a third, only one talent. The master was gone for a long time, but when he returned he went to see how well his servants had invested his money. The master was pleased to find that the servant entrusted with five talents had doubled his investment. Likewise, the servant entrusted with two talents delivered a 100 percent gain. To each of these the master replied, "Well done, good and faithful servant! You have been faithful with a few things; I will put you in charge of many things. Come and share your master's happiness!" (vv. 21, 23) He recognized their differing abilities and rewarded both for their successes. He then acted by giving them more responsibilities and more privileges.

The servant who had received only one talent failed to obtain any gain on the money entrusted to him. The master chided him severely for his failure. We can surmise that the master believed that this servant had the skills to manage a single talent, but failed miserably because of lack of effort. The parable teaches that God expects diligence from His children in using the differing endowments He has bestowed on them as they wait expectantly for His return. As Jesus says in a similar parable, "From everyone who has been given much, much will be demanded" (Luke 12:48).

We must be careful to entrust "five-talent" people with five-talent responsibilities and those with lesser capacities, lesser loads. Admittedly, this is a tricky proposition. We don't always know what is reasonable to expect from others. Besides, some people respond to challenge with much more enthusiasm than others.

Encouragers must make decisions in offering opportunities to others for growth. If I want my child to learn to use money, I'll give her an allowance or let her earn money around the house. If I want an employee to write a report on his own, I will stay out of his office until he delivers it to me.

Other decisions are more difficult. Should I intervene in my child's argument with her neighbor and divert their attention from the quarrel or run the risk of seeing her get hurt? Should I trust my secretary to remember to type my report by noon or should I remind her and display a lack of confidence in her work management skills? Even though decisions are required, the rewards of actions which instill confidence are tremendous.

DOING THE SMALL THING

Encouraging actions need not be monumental. Doing a good turn for another may be extremely encouraging, particularly when the person is without status or means. Jesus rehearses the eternal benefits of showing social interests throughout His earthly life. In Matthew 25 He extols the importance of grasping opportunities for encouragement which present themselves each day. Specifically He mentions giving food and drink to the hungry and thirsty, showing hospitality to strangers, clothing the needy, nursing the sick, and visiting prisoners. Encouraging other people in any of these ways is essentially the same as encouraging Christ Himself. Likewise, the author of Hebrews reminds us to be generous in our encouragement of strangers because some may be special emissaries from God (Heb. 13:2).

I am often amazed at the encouraging power of small gestures. I can well remember the encouragement afforded me and my wife by monetary gifts when we were struggling through graduate school. The size of the donation seemed inconsequential compared to the visible expression of support for us.

The little things we do are often credited with some of our greatest achievements. Couples often gauge their relationship by the little niceties done for each other. I have found that a card or a spontaneous back scratch does wonders for an evening with my wife. Likewise, it is not uncommon to hear employers point to seemingly trivial behaviors as reasons for hiring one person over another. A phone call to a friend, taxiing someone to church, and rolling up the windows of a car about to be drenched with rain all belong in the catalog of encouraging actions. Let's be sure to practice these easy ones.

BEING THERE

Sometimes the most encouraging actions are not special behaviors, but just the act of being with those who desire our company. This is especially true when someone is going through a crisis or dealing with a traumatic event. The gathering of friends and relatives to support close family members in the event of a death illustrates this point. Mourners can do nothing to bring the dead person back to life, but their companionship is often a great comfort to the survivors.

Being there for another person can be a very powerful encouragement. God's omnipresence is a comfort for us at all times, whether He is sharing in our joys or sustaining us through our trials. This characteristic of God is frequently cited by biblical writers as a tremendous source of encouragement. Kind David wrote of God's presence even when hiding in caves from his enemies. Daniel faced hungry lions knowing that God was by his side. Paul sang while imprisoned because God was there with him. What an encouraging resource!

Often we promise to be there for our friends to share in their various experiences. In reality, we are much more apt to be around when things are going well than when the chips are down. This complaint is often voiced by people undergoing emotional crises. They report that others avoid them and this further deepens the feeling that their situation is critical.

Not surprisingly, counselors are regularly complimented for their willingness to stick with hurting people through the bad times.

This encouraging action does not demand clinical skills, just concern and persistence. When someone is suffering, our first inclination is to rescue him. If the circumstances can be rectified by your intervention, by all means do so. I would be much more encouraged by a firm rope if I were sinking in quicksand than by a kind presence and statements of concern.

However, many situations do not lend themselves to heroic rescues. The people experiencing these circumstances still need our firm and continual support. Sometimes others don't even need words from us, just assurance that we're there. In times of distress, silently hanging in there when the emotional plot thickens is often the most encouraging action possible.

Early in life we learn the importance of someone being there for us and we love and trust them for it. You can always determine the primary caretaker of a child by watching who she seeks out when hurt. You'll also find that she looks for this same person first to share her excitement.

We carry this through to adulthood. Being there for others is a tremendous encouragement and places us first in line to share in their joys as well.

MODELING

Practical applications of encouragement are effective ways to train others in this resource. The body of Christ needs consistent examples to strengthen the resolve of others for encouraging actions. The Apostle Paul recognized the importance of modeling encouragement and reminded the Thessalonians of his example in a letter subsequent to his time with them. "For you know that we dealt with you as a father deals with his own children, *encouraging*, comforting and urging you to live lives worthy of God, who calls you into His kingdom and glory" (1 Thes. 2:11-12).

A significant benefit of modeling encouragement is that persons who learn how to encourage from us usually return this encouragement to us liberally. From us, people can learn to show confidence in others. They can learn to encourage others even after they have failed. They can learn to do small things that often have such large meaning. In times of crisis and need, they can learn to be there for others. And they can become examples for other willing pupils who need only a few encouraging experiences to become encouragers themselves.

8.
It's OK
to Feel Good

"Just as everything we said to you was true, so our boasting about you to Titus has proved to be true as well" *(2 Corinthians 7:14).*

The Fourth of July in the United States—what a joyous occasion. The scenery is painted in red, white, and blue, and Old Glory flies from every available flagpole. Bands march to John Philip Sousa's "Stars and Stripes Forever" and we offer renditions of "The Star Spangled Banner." Revolutionary War battles are reenacted and we light the entire sky with fireworks to celebrate our country's victory in her stand for independence and personal freedom. We look with pride upon the accomplishments of our forefathers and commemorate their sacrifices.

We regularly celebrate victories of lesser magnitude as well. Athletic champions are honored by tickertape parades and proclamations of special days commemorating their accomplishments are read. We pay special tribute to those couples who for fifty years have weathered life's storms together, shared its joys, and persevered in those many neutral times in between. Indeed, it is uplifting to celebrate successes with others.

Celebrating victories is not unique to America or the twentieth century, but is characteristic of all societies throughout recorded history. The Bible is filled with accounts of celebrations of God's goodness to His people. In fact, explicit instructions for national celebrations are detailed throughout the Old Testament. For instance, God's care for His children during the Exodus was noted every year through the Passover and the Feast of Tabernacles. New Testament Christians celebrate Jesus Christ's victory over death through His resurrection at Easter and in services each Sunday, the day He arose. These actions honor God and direct attention to His expressions of love to His children. These commemorations encourage us as we recognize the Lord's benevolence and constant concern.

Victory celebrations renew our faith in the persons or institutions being honored. They remind us of the risks taken by the victors and the fortitude exerted to succeed. They challenge us to exercise the skills modeled by the victors and empower us with resolve to attempt the same feats.

PERSONAL CELEBRATIONS

Honoring personal successes is no less rewarding than recognizing national and religious ones. These celebrations build confidence. Through them we review the steps taken to gain the victory, relive the emotions associated with our actions at each stage, and reexperience the gratifying feelings of success. This process encourages us to take future risks and builds expectations of similar positive outcomes.

My daughter, Kristen (age 6), recently learned to ride her bicycle without its training wheels. Although this may seem like a mundane feat to you, it was a personal triumph for her and a cause for celebration in our family. Last year I taught

Kristen to ride without her training wheels and she learned the necessary skills immediately. But on her second solo trip that fateful day, she forgot to brake and ran into a parked car. From that moment on, she insisted that the training wheels be returned to their supportive roles.

The problem for Kristen was that her peers had all learned to ride their bicycles without training wheels. They were pressuring her to do the same. A concerned neighborhood girl asked my daughter why she continued to use her training wheels. Kristen replied that she would abandon them at the ripe age of eight. The girl then warned my daughter, "You'd better learn to ride without them now or the kids will make fun of you."

That little girl's honest feedback did more to motivate my daughter than a year's worth of cajoling from me. You see, Kristen has always been apprehensive to try any task which has even a remote possibility of personal injury or discomfort. Yet that very afternoon, Kristen took the risks that had seemed so foreboding and became accomplished at bike-riding very quickly.

Although I did not arrive home until after dark on the landmark day, my daughter awaited me anxiously and demonstrated her new skill thoroughly that night. She rehearsed every detail of her self-instruction that afternoon and beamed as I applauded her mastery of her fear. I encouraged her to retell the whole story several times and watched her confidence level rise with each recollection. She went to bed eagerly anticipating the next day when she would demonstrate her success again and again.

Kristen's heroics highlight several features of personal victory celebrations. The most obvious is that success is gratifying and breeds future success. Retelling her success escalated personal confidence to the extent that there was no question that she would engage in the behavior again. My job was to encourage this reliving of her thrilling afternoon even though the techniques she used and the experiences she underwent were hardly news to me.

Not to be forgotten is the power of one discouraging experience. My daughter had denied herself the exhilaration of riding a bicycle for a whole year because of one failure. She had repeatedly relived her failure and its outcome despite reassurances and offers to help her overcome the problem. It's a shame that our defeats receive such a disproportionate amount of play time in the airwaves of our minds.

SUCCESS

"Nothing succeeds like success." This often quoted maxim contains a great deal of truth. Albert Bandura, a noted psychologist at Stanford University, has extensively researched the factors which influence self-confidence. He found that previous experiences in handling personal demands is the most significant source of information we use to gauge our present capabilities."

People who have a good track record of successes have positive confidence levels. They are willing to hang in there when immediate results aren't forthcoming and can weather numerous obstacles to their goals. They are more likely to be rewarded with success again because of their persistence. From their past experiences, they learn which actions are more likely to succeed. This further increases their effectiveness and confidence.

My mentor, Dr. Ken Matheny, is an excellent example of a successful person. He was raised in a family with few material and educational advantages, but this did not deter him from setting high standards and expending the effort to reach them. During his entire life he has been willing to take the risks necessary to learn new things. Each of these steps was inevitably rewarded with success which, in turn, provided the confidence for a new venture. His resume bulges with prestigious accomplishments. He holds the rank of Regents Professor at his University and he is a favorite among students who flock to his classes year after year. He is perhaps the most encouraging person I know. His success is the result of persistence which translated into many small successes and ultimately large ones.

People who regard themselves as failures tend to dwell on their perceived inadequacies, creating a paralysis which inhibits movement toward their goals. When any obstacle is encountered, they tend to give up easily. This discourages them further and makes success even more elusive. These people lack self-confidence and make this apparent to all those around them. They are in dire need of encouragement from others who can spot their successful strivings and throw a "victory celebration" for them.

BUT IS THIS BIBLICAL?

A frequent objection to encouragement through celebrating victories is that it may breed prideful persons who fail to recognize God's role in their successes. This is rarely the case. Encouraged Christians are actually more likely to recognize God's influence on their lives because they are freed from the pervasive doubts that plague noncelebrants. Their successes further impress them with the significance of their Heavenly Resource and empower them with the confidence to encourage others in the body of Christ.

The Apostle Paul encouraged others by celebrating victories liberally. The first-century Corinthian church was beset by numerous pagan influences which often found their way into the local assembly. Paul's letters to the Corinthians were packed with instruction on sound doctrine and practical Christian living. But even in the midst of woeful problems, Paul readily acknowledged their successful strivings. In his second letter to them he recounted his heartfelt sorrow in scolding these believers in a previous letter. Yet he also recognized their success in dealing with the matter. Paul celebrated this victory excitedly with these believers:

> I have great confidence in you; I take great pride in you. I am greatly encouraged; in all our troubles my joy knows no bounds.... In addition to our own encouragement, we were especially delighted to see how happy Titus was, because his spirit has been refreshed by all of you. I had boasted to him about you, and you have not embarrassed me. But just as everything we said to you was true, so our boasting about you to Titus has proved to be true as well. And his affection for you is all the greater when he remembers that you were all obedient, receiving him with fear and trembling. I am glad I can have complete confidence in you (2 Cor. 7:13-16).

In similar fashion Paul celebrates the Thessalonians' faith and steadfastness. He states plainly, "In all our distress and persecution we were encouraged about you because of your faith.... How can we thank God enough for you in return for all the joy we have in the presence of our God because of you?" (1 Thes. 3:7, 9) These Christians evidenced positive behaviors and attitudes. Paul was happy to encourage their success and acknowledge how they had richly encouraged him as well.

HOW TO CELEBRATE VICTORIES WITH OTHERS

Get in the Spirit of Celebration. It's hard to celebrate when we aren't really up for it. That's why our attitudes are first on the checklist in this practical section. No one can be expected to feel on top of the world all the time and we can't expect to feel like encouraging others in this way constantly. If a person has a toothache, it will be difficult to redirect his focus from the pain in his mouth to the behaviors of others. But this is understandable. Ignoring our own life situations in favor of any technique usually smacks of phoniness and this is hardly encouraging. My main concern is our *general* attitudes toward others and the amount of permission we give ourselves to engage in these skills in normal life circumstances.

There are two major attitudinal barriers to encouragement through celebrating successes. The first is an unwillingness to be *for* others. Some people do not celebrate with others because they are not happy about another's successes. Instead, they are critical constantly. When someone fails, they are close at hand with an "I told you it would never work." When someone succeeds, they are nowhere to be found.

This attitude of being against others can be a deep-seated characterological trait, but often it is simply a learned behavior which can be changed. It is the stuff of which rivalries are made and it can degenerate to unfriendly terms.

During my junior year in college I saw the ugliness of this phenomenon develop. In the dormitory I lived with people from all across the United States. We generally got along well with one another and were mutually friendly and encouraging. However, when basketball season arrived, a lot of dissension came with it. Each of us took pride in our home states and regularly extolled the heroics of our state's most successful college basketball program.

Soon our friendly discussions became argumentative. We were using the performances of people who didn't even know us (the basketball players) to show our personal superiority. When my team lost, I was not to be found. When my team won, I was not to be shut up. Soon we began cheering for any opponent to beat each others' teams. This was taking place *while* most of us played together on an intramural basketball team and *while* we attended our own college's basketball games together. We were all on the same side during those contests.

As the basketball season dragged on, our confrontations in the dorm became more heated and our attitudes became more bitter. We found it hard to appreciate anything that our fellow students did. We had been transformed from persons who were basically *for* each other into adversaries who were intensely *against* one another. And all of this was over a silly game that was totally out of our control.

I learned a number of things from this experience. Most significantly, no one is immune from developing negative attitudes toward others. It happened to me and my class-mates over a trivial matter. I also learned that once I took a stance against others in even one area, my capacity to celebrate their successes in *any* area diminished tremen-dously. And since the team from North Carolina (my home state) failed to win the national title that year, I also learned the hazards of basing my self-esteem on the actions of people who didn't know I existed. I also learned that these negative attitudes did not need to persist. Indeed, they were quite amenable to change once I decided to dispense with the foolishness.

The other attitudinal barrier to encouragement through celebrating successes is a fear that it is unscriptural. Some people see this type of encouragement as a means of stealing God's glory for our accomplishments. They believe that per-sonal victory celebrations will serve only to puff the success-ful person up with pride and create a totally self-sufficient attitude.

In reality, this fear is rarely realized. Rehearsals of suc-cessful experiences usually have the opposite effect. We tend to recognize God's empowering even more as we re-count our actions. But feeling good about ourselves is hardly problematic. God grants special abilities and skills to each of His children and *expects* us to cultivate them and use them for His glory. In fact, this is what constitutes a truly successful experience in the first place. Remember Paul's admonitions to build up one another and his example of boasting about the successes of his converts.

Failure to be *for* others is essentially selfishness. And selfishness is a sin. If we are to encourage others in any way, we must modify our selfish attitudes. Failure to celebrate with others on scriptural grounds is unfounded and is in stark disobedience to the multiple New Testament commands to build up one another. Once we straighten out our thinking, we should be in the mood to celebrate!

Look for Success. Now that we are willing to acknowledge the successes of others, we must search for the appropriate victories to celebrate. Some will be easily spotted. Graduation from college, setting Sunday School attendance records, and landing a lucrative business account are readily recognizable successes.

However, most of our victories are much more mundane. Speaking up in a Bible study may be a major accomplishment for a shy parishioner, but it may go virtually unnoticed by the other nonfearful participants. Learning the Apostle's Creed is typically celebrated when accomplished by children, but the same action by an adult may draw little applause.

These seemingly small successes are the ones that are more desperate for our encouragement, since the larger ones gain celebration naturally. Jesus was always willing to acknowledge those small victories which others frequently overlooked. For example, He extolled the importance of providing a thirsty person with a cup of cold water (Matt. 10:42), and celebrated the wisdom of Mary's choice to commune with Him instead of preparing His dinner (Luke 10:38-42). Perhaps Jesus' most memorable celebration of a seemingly small success is recorded in Mark 12 where the small offering of a humble widow was applauded more loudly than the larger gifts of the wealthy (vv. 41-44).

Often the successes that appear so insignificant to others

are the most rewarding to us. Any parent who has struggled to toilet train a small child knows the elation associated with a task generally considered routine. Likewise, an adult who foregoes dessert in the interest of maintaining a slim waist-line achieves a personally significant goal. Whether by slipping a candy into the child's mouth or patting the adult's back, these small efforts at establishing self-control deserve a victory celebration.

Some persons are not very successful at the tasks they try. Even their small successes are often overlooked because of the overall negative outcome. But in their failure, some glimmer of positive striving may be detected. Celebrating a move in the right direction may lead to further striving and eventual success. Therefore, be ready to acknowledge *any* steps in the right direction.

Recount the Success. Victory celebrations may consist of a mere acknowledgment of success. However, the most effective celebrations allow the victor to recount the steps to his success and the events surrounding it. After a pro football game we often see interviews with victorious athletes who are being shown replays of their heroic moments and asked for commentary on their performances.

We enjoy reliving our successes and encouragers must be willing to allow these re-creations. In fact, we should solicit them and join in the enthusiasm of the victor.

Give God His Place in the Success. Christians realize that all gifts and abilities come ultimately from God. Victory celebrations which leave God out are clearly deficient. Whoever heard of a superbowl champion football team minimizing their coach's role in the victory? On the other hand, spiritualizing every accomplishment with clichés such as "I just let go and let God" seem contrived and overlook the instrument that God empowered with special abilities and gifts to complete the task at hand.

We must strike a balance in our encouragement. All victories are within the ultimate permissive will of God, but a statement to this effect is rarely received as an encouraging remark. Instead, acknowledgment of God's granting of a resource and someone's successful implementation of that resource is much more encouraging. A statement such as, "You've really developed your God-given potential and it shows in your success today" strikes a balance, giving God His glory and encouraging the believer.

Celebration as Feedback. We often progress at a slow pace which makes recognizing our growth difficult. Remember how, as a child during your yearly visit with Aunt Karen and Uncle Bob, they would always comment that you had "grown like a weed" in such a short time? Yet you could never detect any change in your stature at all. In the same way, people will frequently be unaware of their spiritual and emotional advances which seem obvious to others.

Giving feedback concerning our views of the changes in others is a potent way to celebrate a victory they may not have recognized themselves. This is a common occurrence in psychotherapy. I will talk to a person about her progress and she seems oblivious to any positive changes. I have often wished aloud in a counseling session that I had a videotape of my first encounter with the person to use for comparison purposes. But in the absence of a portrait captured on film, recounting the specific behavioral and attitudinal changes usually points out the gains achieved.

When giving feedback, it is most helpful to focus on observable changes rather than on global ones. For example, telling someone, "Your self-esteem has improved" is more helpful when we add, "I've noticed that you give good eye contact and assert yourself more." Feedback celebrations are very meaningful because they demonstrate your special interest in another person.

Helping Success Breed Success. Encouragement through celebration is a marvelous way to perpetuate success and create the need for another victory party in the future. We enjoy the pleasurable experiences of celebrating with others, and this paves the way to even more success. These celebrations instill hope and encourage future risk-taking with the anticipation of success.

The most effective celebrations of success predict future success. It's heartening to hear, "I'm glad you spoke up in Sunday School today." But it's more motivating to hear, "Your insights into the Sunday School lesson were helpful. I hope you'll share some more of them next week."

Even corrective feedback given for only partial successes can be an encouragement for future striving. Its value depends upon one's tone and stated expectation. Corrective feedback that points out an error, but gives no hope for future success is quite discouraging: "No, you've messed it up again. Just call me next time you want to use it." On the other hand, corrective feedback which states an expectation of future success is very encouraging: "Hey, that can happen to anyone. You'll get it next time." Expectations must be kept within realistic boundaries and should be stated clearly when used for encouragement.

Celebrations of success are natural responses to victories. They are potent and rewarding encouragers. We should be quick to follow the Apostle Paul's example of encouraging the successes of fellow believers by looking for things to celebrate and being liberal in these celebrations.

9.
Say "Thank You" and Mean It

"Therefore each of you must put off falsehood and speak truthfully to his neighbor" (Ephesians 4:25).

For such a universally desired commodity, encouragement is greeted with a wide variety of responses. Reactions range from a sheepish "Oh, it was nothing" to a bold "Thanks, I really do that well." Most people seem a bit embarrassed by encouraging comments. No doubt you've come into contact with an encouragement-deprived individual. When this starving person receives even a small morsel of positive feedback, he soaks it up like a dehydrated sponge. Others may say absolutely nothing when complimented.

Just what is the proper way to receive encouragement? In this chapter we will investigate responses to encouragement and the most appropriate ways to handle them.

ACCEPTING ENCOURAGEMENT

It's OK to accept encouragement! However, many persons have difficulty with this proposition. Let's put it another way:

If God has given a biblical blueprint for encouraging, it must be appropriate to accept it when encountered.

Though we crave encouragement from others, we often do not know how to respond to it. Researchers have found that most people who receive compliments feel uncomfortable and have a hard time responding to their encourager.[10] We often fear that the acknowledgment of a compliment is a prideful act, even if we believe the compliment is true. Social convention sometimes dictates that we cannot accept praise. It is tragic to reject the encouragements of others because they are so uplifting.

We fear accepting praise for other reasons. Some are concerned that acknowledgment of a compliment is an evidence of conceit. If I say, "I thought I did a good job too," I might be seen as a haughty individual. Sometimes we have trouble accepting compliments because we don't want to appear superior to the person who gives the compliment. In these cases one might reply, "Well, I sure wish that I could do it as well as you can." At other times we resist accepting compliments because it may be hard to live up to the compliment in the future. If someone says to me, "You're really an excellent tennis player," I may now have added pressure on me the next time I go to the courts. If I deny the compliment, I may alleviate some of this pressure.

This reasoning breaks down under close examination. People who spurn compliments for fear of acting prideful often cite verses such as Proverbs 27:2, "Let another praise you, and not your own mouth," to support this refusal. The verse does not condemn one for accepting praise, but rather for prominently "tooting his own horn."

Embarrassment is usually a learned response which can be unlearned simply through practice. Anytime we try out something new, from a pair of shoes to a new golf swing, it feels uncomfortable. But after some experience, it begins to feel natural. If we've learned to act embarrassed when complimented, other responses will seem uncomfortable until we've "broken them in."

The way we accept praise and compliments from others strongly relates to our self-esteem. We are much more likely to accept a compliment if it fits with our own personal evaluations of ourselves. In every case our perceptions of our abilities are more important than how well we really performed. For instance, if I believe that I am a good public speaker and someone compliments me after a speaking engagement, I am likely to respond, "Thank you. I'm glad you liked it." On the other hand, if I believe that I am a poor public speaker and someone approaches me after a speech and says, "I really enjoyed your presentation tonight," I would be more likely to reply, "You're very kind. I am glad you endured it."

Persons with positive self-esteem are more likely to believe that they do a good job. They recognize that they are not perfect, but are willing to look at their good points as well as their bad ones. They tend to be more realistic in their perceptions of themselves. All this adds up to a greater willingness to accept compliments and praise. The person with poor self-esteem is suspicious of the compliments of others. This person is less willing to accept encouragement because he does not believe that he deserves it. Instead of saying simply, "Thank you," to an encouraging remark, the person with poor self-esteem engages in self-abasement ("Oh, anyone could have done it.").

WHEN WE FAIL TO ACCEPT ENCOURAGEMENT

Though usually done out of some sense of humility, failure to accept encouraging remarks from others may have several negative effects. Failure to accept a compliment can bring the encourager's judgment into question. If someone says, "I love the way you decorated your house," and we reply, "Oh, I think it's just so ordinary," we are making a critical statement about the complimentor's taste. This reluctance to accept a compliment can be seen as an affront to the complimentor.

When someone gives us a sincere and honest encouraging remark and we downplay it, we may hurt their feelings. I will never forget an occasion when I made this terrible mistake. I had worked very hard on a project in one of my classes in graduate school and had received a good grade for my work. After the class period in which the project was returned, I walked up to a group of friends, only one of whom was taking the course with me. As soon as I arrived my classmate said, "You did a great job on that project. I know you put a lot of work into it." Instead of thanking him for his thoughtfulness, I downplayed his compliment. I said, "Oh, it really wasn't that difficult. I only put a few hours in it anyway," even though this was a drastic minimization of the time and effort it took to complete the project. My encourager became quiet and the group went on to talk about other matters. Later I discovered that just before I joined the group, my classmate had told the others the difficulty of the assigned project. He described the hours and hours of intensive work it had taken him to complete his project. My terse comments—though meant to minimize self-glory—were very insulting to my classmate. I had effectively told the group that my classmate was incompetent for devoting such a significant amount of time to an easy project. My comments implied that he was rather stupid.

When we downplay their encouragement, people respond in several ways. Some reassert their compliment in stronger terms after our denial. This usually results in another downplay of the compliment and the cycle goes on until someone tires. This is often uncomfortable and is clearly a needless communication pattern. Others simply learn not to encourage you. They may see your disclaimers as ploys to garner further praise and decide to avoid this manipulation. Or they may feel punished since you are implying that they have poor taste or that they are lying. In any case, you may actually train others to ignore your accomplishments and thus sidestep an uncomfortable exchange with you.

Questions of integrity arise when we discount the encouragement of others. Attempts at modesty such as, "Oh, it was nothing," are often quite untruthful. In reality, we may have spent a considerable amount of time on a particular task and our success is attributable to this hard work. This is *something!* Disclaimers such as "Anyone could have done it," are rarely accurate. We may have special talents and skills in an area that can't be matched proficiently by others. Frankly, many of our discounting remarks are lies. Our frequent disclaimers to others are merely polite ways of calling our encourager a liar. This is hardly the desired effect and it certainly is not a biblically directed response.

Failure to accept encouragement also undermines our self-esteem. We might use personal disclaimers of our performance to convince ourselves that indeed we did an inadequate job. Most of us have seen this attempt at modesty backfire. We are given a compliment such as, "Wow, you really put a lot of time into this work and it looks great!" We might respond with, "Well, it wasn't that hard. I'm sure anyone could have done it." Then the encourager says, "Oh, I thought it was difficult. I guess not." Now we have downplayed our own performance in another's eyes and they have changed their perceptions of us. A steady diet of this discounting will ultimately serve to deflate our own assessments of our performance.

TYPICAL RESPONSES TO COMPLIMENTS

Some researchers[11] have analyzed the content of our replies to compliments. They categorized these replies into general and subcategories. The first category, *acceptance*, has three forms. We may accept compliments in a ritualistic way with a simple "Thank you" and a smile. We may also accept compliments and show our pleasure in receiving them. Or we may accept compliments yet demonstrate embarrassment.

Another category of replies to compliments is *acceptance accompanied by an amendment*. We may accept the compliment from another, but add a diminishing phrase to this acceptance like, "Thanks, but I've got a long way to go." At other times we respond to a compliment by returning it to the complimentor. We may amend acceptance by actually magnifying the compliment, usually in an effort to seem humorous. One might say, "You bet. I'm the best typist in the world." Sometimes we may try to gain more information than the complimentor offered. An example of this response is, "Oh, really? What did you like about it?"

The third category of compliment replies is really failure to reply at all. Though this is rare, some persons totally ignore the compliments of another. This response is an outright denial or contradiction of the praise given by another.

HOW TO ACCEPT ENCOURAGEMENT

The most appropriate response to a compliment is a simple "Thank you." There's no need to engage in long explanations for your actions or give a detailed history of how you came to make the response you made. This is often boring and causes the encourager to doubt the wisdom of his decision to compliment you.

Responding "Thank you" to compliments saves us from attempts at false humility and keeps us from downplaying our performances. It affirms the encourager's judgment in complimenting us in the first place, unlike disclaimers which make the encourager scramble to reassert his observation or make it more palatable.

We benefit the most when we greet compliments with simple thanks. This reply frees us to enjoy the encouragement without worrying about composing a long response. It allows us to focus on the encourager instead of concerning ourselves with how we're coming across to the complimentor. It allows us to be concise. And best of all, it is simple to learn and almost universally applicable in our culture.

See for yourself. Say "Thank you" once or twice and that's all the practice you need to learn to accept encouragement. Now comes the harder part. You must replace your characteristic way of responding with these simple words. This may take more effort, but it should be well worth the energy.

Likewise, care should be taken to accept corrective feedback given by others with simple thanks. The Book of Proverbs is filled with directives to heed the counsel of significant others. "Listen to advice and accept instruction, and in the end you will be wise" (Prov. 19:20). "Instruct a wise man and he will be wiser still; teach a righteous man and he will add to his learning" (9:9).

Honest feedback from caring friends should be received with gracious thanks. If you need clarification or more information, it is quite acceptable to ask for this; however, defensive comments should be offered only after careful consideration of the facts. We do not want to punish others for taking the risks necessary to encourage us in this way.

SELF-ENCOURAGEMENT

After we learn to accept compliments from others we must learn to accept encouragement from ourselves. Since all of our experience is filtered through our own personal perceptions, any encouragement received ultimately must be accepted and passed on to us through what we say to ourselves. In this way, our self-talk is the gatekeeper of all encouragement. If I am praised for doing something I really had no hand in accomplishing, I will not feel encouraged even if I do not inform the encourager that I deserve no credit. In the same way, I will receive little encouragement from an insincere compliment because I tell myself that it is not a true representation of the other person's feelings. However, if I'm not careful, I may discount a sincere compliment from another merely by talking myself out of it. It is essential to train our gatekeepers—our personal perceptions and self-talk—to be open to encouraging remarks and honest evaluations from others.

Self-encouragement goes beyond accepting the endorsements of others. It also involves learning to endorse ourselves. Of course, this does not mean that we should invent reasons to tell ourselves we're OK or praise ourselves for every move we make. Rather, it is appraising our performances realistically and giving ourselves credit for successes when credit is due.

Accepting self-encouragement does not mean that we downplay God's contribution to our actions or set ourselves up as flawless individuals. It does mean that we learn to endorse ourselves just as positively as God endorses us so that we are not totally dependent upon the recognition of others for encouragement. The most healthy model is the person who freely accepts encouragement from God, others, and himself. This is the formula for success.

10.
Children and Encouragement

"But Jesus called the children to Him and said, 'Let the little children come to Me, and do not hinder them, for the kingdom of God belongs to such as these'" (Luke 18:16).

"Look, Daddy! Look, Daddy!" exclaimed little Jimmie as he ran into the house clutching a paper tightly in his fist. "My teacher said...."

"Jimmie, move. I can't see the TV through you," said Jimmie's father. "And be sure to shut that door tightly."

Jimmie ran back and checked the door, stood out of the direct line of vision to the television and then said, "Dad, my teacher really liked the science project I turned in. She said that it may have a chance to win a prize at the state science show."

"That's nice, Jimmie," responded his father with his eyes fixed on the evening news. "Have you seen your sister?"

This is a scene which occurs every day. Our most precious resources, our children, play second fiddle to somebody else. Many times this somebody else is not even a person we know. Opportunities that are ripe for encouraging remarks go unnoticed and our children are fed a diet of discouragement.

THE ENCOURAGING PARENT

"How should I raise my children? I mean, what can I do to make sure they turn out all right?" Visit any maternity ward and you will hear variations of this question. It is regularly put to psychologists, pediatricians, educators, and pastors.

We recognize a grave responsibility to our children. We have to train them and we want to do it right. In fact, if something goes wrong with our child, we look first to ourselves for an explanation. When the condition of an emotionally troubled college student necessitates a call to his parents, their lament is inevitably offered, "We raised him the best we knew how. I wonder where we failed?"

Parenting is a tall order. Advice is available from numerous sources. Your local Christian and secular booksellers have shelves lined with strategies for this undertaking. People, especially those *without* children, are always happy to give their opinions. We are often deluged with advice which is usually idealistic and sometimes contradictory.

You are not a perfect parent and neither am I. But I am concerned that we use our opportunities every day to encourage our children. As they grow and mature, our children will forgive us for imperfections. Yet they may harbor grudges well into adulthood if we don't try to encourage them.

ENCOURAGE THEM EARLY

Encouragement is a vital resource for children in their developmental years. It plays a very important role in their social, spiritual, mental, and emotional growth, and can have lasting positive effects which will be drawn upon throughout their lives. Because of its significant influence on self-esteem, encouragement may be the most crucial parenting skill we can master.

The need to belong is very basic, shared by persons everywhere. It is first recognized in our families as we struggle through infancy and childhood. As children, we fervently seek our place in the family as we jockey for parental attention and learn to relate to siblings and the outside world. When this is negotiated successfully, we enjoy positive adjustment and good mental health. When we encounter difficulties in this early search for belonging, discouragement results which can foster a myriad of dysfunctional behaviors and attitudes. Discouraged children often adopt devious and self-defeating behaviors in their attempts to fit in and gain attention. Adults call this *misbehavior.*

Psychiatrist Rudolf Dreikurs traces all childhood misbehavior to four goals: gaining attention, seeking power over others, taking revenge on those who mistreat them, and securing nurturance by flaunting presumed personal inadequacies.[12] If discouragement continues into adolescence and adulthood, the patterns may develop into characteristic methods of relating to others and become more complex and well entrenched. Early encouragement is the most promising antidote to this problem.

Children need encouragement in the broadest sense of the word. All of the methods previously detailed in this book are indicated but special attention should be given to the following areas: accepting the child as he is, demonstrating faith in his abilities, and building his strengths.

ACCEPTING YOUR CHILD AS HE IS

Getting on Your Child's Level. Just watching a child provides a good deal of encouragement, but optimal levels of encouragement demand more work. The attending skills outlined in chapter 3 work very well with children since youngsters are quite tuned in to nonverbal forms of communication. It is extremely important to face the child fully, lean forward, maintain almost constant eye contact, and refrain from distracting behaviors. Encouraging adults must get on the child's level—not in personal maturity, but in height and vocabulary. Children are small and spend a great deal of time looking up to adults. Effective encouragers recognize the barriers that height differences pose and overcome these by holding children in their laps or getting on the floor to be nearer to children.

Attending need not be a solemn or austere behavior. When Kristen was two years old, we embarked on a Bible memory program. Working together at the kitchen table was disastrous. Kristen could not sit quietly for any length of time and I'm sure I was showing more interest in the Bible verses than in my daughter. So I asked her what she'd like to do. She suggested jumping on the bed (a permissible activity in our home). I sat, legs crossed on the bed, leaning forward, watching my daughter intently as she jumped and laughed. Kristen was soaking up my attention and enjoying herself.

Then an amazing thing occurred. She began attempting the Bible verses that had bored her only minutes before. She repeated the words after me in a sing-song voice that corresponded to her jumping movements. Soon we were spending many sessions on the bed jumping and learning as she memorized a good number of Bible verses. Interestingly, Kristen rarely jumped on the bed when I was not watching her. The whole activity had entertainment value only when I attended and then the educational element was welcomed.

Children love attention, especially the attention of adults. They want to be noticed, to have a turn, to hear a compliment. They want you to watch them. Attending to our children opens communication lines. Children are more willing both to talk and to listen when we are paying attention to them. Sadly, most kids are starving for this kind of encouragement.

Entering Their Worlds. A child's world is prioritized much differently than an adult's. Finding the red crayon or buttoning his own shirt may be the most important task of the day. Therefore, empathy (understanding the child's world through the child's eyes) is a critical task. We must take the time to view things from the child's perspective instead of merely filtering them through our own. Only after we reach this understanding can we respond encouragingly to the child.

Recently we were traveling back home to Indiana after spending a few weeks in North Carolina with my parents. Anna, our three-year-old daughter, had been playing happily with a small doll which had been given to her earlier that morning by her dear, doting grandmother. From her back-seat car chair, Anna momentarily stuck the baby doll's little head out the small door vent. The wind whisked the doll's pink hat right off her head.

Anna became quite distressed about the wind's cruelty and began crying. Soon I ascertained the scope of the trage-dy through my daughter's sobbing words. She had a single answer to this predicament: "Daddy, turn the car around and go back and get my baby's hat."

Simple, right? I was to stop the car and comb a five-mile strip of four-lane interstate highway for a pink baby doll hat which measured one inch in diameter. Needless to say, I took a slightly different perspective than my daughter of the gravity of our loss and kept motoring down the highway.

Then I made my error. I tried to convince Anna that it was no big deal. I told her that the doll was worth only a few bucks and the hat was quite an expendable article of cloth-ing. We had a long trip ahead of us and stopping would only increase our travel time. Besides, we'd never find the hat anyway.

I was 100 percent accurate and extremely rational in my explanation. I was also very discouraging. I had failed totally to empathize with my brokenhearted daughter. From her perspective, the doll was a priceless treasure from her beloved grandmother. Now it was hatless, defaced forever. My daughter needed empathy, not the cold facts. I should have said, "I know you're sad because your baby's hat is gone. You don't think she will ever be the same." Now I've entered Anna's world and shown that I understand her grief. Although I still don't stop the car, we now can explore her feelings and it may provide an excellent opportunity to discuss life's inevitable disappointments. I could have been encouraging!

It is essential that we suspend our own frame of reference when talking with children in order to gain their perspective. The obstacles which seem so foreboding to them often seem little more than annoyances from our perspective. The adolescent's depression precipitated by the first sign of a pimple may seem a bit exaggerated from our point of view. Likewise, the joys of children may be quite different from ours. The preschooler's ecstatic reaction to the prize in a fastfood lunch may not elicit a comparable response from us. We will hardly adopt their perspective as our own, but we must acknowledge it if we are to encourage them.

DEMONSTRATING FAITH IN YOUR CHILD'S ABILITY

Those Encouraging Words. Compliments are an obvious source of encouragement to our children. Young people thrive on praise just as do adults. Even recognition for small successes such as, "You colored that picture well," if given sincerely are great encouragers. Likewise, thanking our children for the things they do can have very positive effects.

Sadly, most adults are for more proficient at distributing criticism than compliments. It's easy to recognize the bicycle left in the driveway, the crayon marks on the bedroom wall, and the fresh scratch on the car. Indeed, these issues usually need to be addressed and discipline may need to be introduced to correct misbehavior. But let's face it, our children do far more things right than wrong.

Of course, it is unfeasible and impossible to compliment every single appropriate behavior of our children. Yet it is especially important to comment positively on corrected behavior that has drawn your criticism in the past. If you reproved your teenage son yesterday for blasting your eardrums with the stereo speakers, be sure to compliment his more polite operation of the volume control today. If your three-year-old's mismanagement of the crayon box has drawn your very pointed directives in the past, don't forget to pronounce her efforts to put them away "well done!"

As a rule of thumb, you should compliment a task performed successfully at least three times for every time you criticize its inadequate performance. The problem is that most of us fail to recognize how often we are critical. We drastically underestimate our fault-finding. It takes a significant amount of concentration on your communications with your children to detect these. It is sometimes necessary to have your spouse help monitor your criticisms and cue you as to their frequency and to your children's appropriate behavior which deserves commendation. In some cases this discouraging process can be conteracted only by stringently recording your critical remarks and checking off each time you encourage your child for subsequent successful performance on the task which was criticized. This cumbersome task may be necessary for a day or two to get the new habit pattern started.

Compliments need not revolve around performance. Children are greatly encouraged by our affirmations of them just for being our children. Statements such as "Kristen, I love you. I'm really glad you're my daughter," or "It's great to have you for my son, Andy," are very effective in building our children up and enhancing self-esteem. (They work equally well with our spouses.) These compliments are especially encouraging when our children are not doing something spectacular. These affirmations demonstrate unconditional love and appreciation for our kids.

Encourage Risk-Taking. "Go ahead and try, Son. I think you can do it." This type of encouragement is perhaps the most needed by our children. Self-confidence is instilled through success experiences which can occur only when risks are taken. Life consists of challenges and effective adjustment requires proficiency in meeting them. Children who develop confidence in their abilities to handle life's demands enjoy a valuable resource which will pay handsome dividends throughout life.

Parents can play a pivotal role in encouraging their children's risk-taking behaviors. Children naturally feel small and inferior, given their relative size and ability levels when compared to adults. Parents may easily exacerbate these feelings and hinder the development of self-confidence by several modes of discouragement. Obviously, acts of hatred and rejection by parents send a clear message that the child is unworthy. But the other extreme is equally discouraging. Overindulgence and overprotectiveness send the message that the parents lack faith in their child's abilities and create misgivings in the child.

The most encouraging response is a balanced one. Effective parents encourage the initiative of their child and guarantee acceptance. Parents should never do for their child what he can to for himself. Letting the child develop a feeling of independence cultivates a rewarding sense of self-confidence. The trick is discovering the optimal match between the child's abilities and a comparable task. The best gauge of this match is the child's emotional reaction. Interest and mild surprise indicate a good match.

Encourage Persistence. Sometimes a child will give up easily if he runs into any obstacle. Adults need to encourage persistence when they are confident that the task falls within the child's capabilities. Persistence is a result of previous success in handling a task, minimal frustration levels, and immediate reinforcement.

Two of the most difficult tasks of my growing-up years were learning to tie my shoes as a preschooler and my necktie as an early adolescent. Making a few loops in a shoelace in those pre-Velcro days was very frustrating. My first attempts at this elusive goal were disastrous. Fortunately, my mother was a patient teacher. She showed me the steps repeatedly and celebrated every approximation to a bow. I was able to build on my success, muster the energy to deal with mild frustration, and receive immediate feedback and reinforcement. This formula led to persistence and eventual success.

Learning to tie a necktie was another frustrating task. I clearly had the skills to negotiate a knot in the necktie, but I wasn't encouraged to persist after my failures. My father dutifully demonstrated the appropriate technique, but he was not blessed with my mother's patience. After five or six ill-fated attempts at tying the knot, he suggested that I let him tie it. He could slip it over his head and onto my neck. Later I could unloosen it gently and hang it on the rack, knot neatly in place, for the next time I needed to wear it.

I had no past success to build upon, and I began to perceive the task as insurmountable. I lost confidence every time I thought about tying my necktie. This went on for over two years until I devoted myself to the chore of learning to tie the knot because my inadequacy was becoming embarrassing. Even now I still dislike tying a necktie and it usually takes me two tries to get it right. My early failure to be persistent carried a high price tag.

Reframing a Threat as a Challenge. Another way to

encourage risk-taking is to help your child view a new thing as a challenge instead of a threat. Our emotional response to any event is directly attributable to what we say to ourselves about the event. As John Milton put it in *Paradise Lost,* "The mind is its own place, and in itself can make a heaven of hell, or a hell of heaven." The same idea is offered in Proverbs 23:7, "As [a man] thinketh in his heart, so is he" (KJV). Our view of an event is critical.

Children react to their worlds according to their interpretations of events and these interpretations are gleaned largely from their parents. If we respond positively to educational activities, chances are that our children will also value them. If we give our pastor negative reviews at Sunday dinner, our children will probably hold him in lower esteem as well. Parents hold a powerful position in influencing their children's perceptions.

This phenomenon has a number of implications for parenting. I'd like to zero in on its impact on encouraging risk-taking. Children will try new things only if they feel safe doing so. If we paint a bleak picture of the world and forecast the failure of any new venture, our children will dutifully stay safely on home base and refuse to tackle a new task. If we encourage exploration by predicting success, our children will have much more energy to attempt something new. It is important to frame new things as challenges rather than threats. We enjoy a challenge and can endure frustrations when pursuing one, but a threat is scary and discouraging.

Almost any activity can be viewed as either a challenge or a threat. If a nine-foot giant hurled insults at us and promised bodily harm, most of us would consider this a clear threat. However, a teenaged boy named David labeled this behavior a challenge and responded by risking everything in his ultimate defeat of Goliath. Answering a question in a group, learning to swim, even petting a dog can be viewed as a challenge or a threat. Encouraging parents frame new experiences in positive terms to highlight the challenging aspects and encourage risk-taking. Once action is initiated with an expectant attitude, success is a real probability.

One day when I was ten years old I went with a neighbor to the first day of swimming team practice in our small town. The coach began the session by opening up team membership to anyone who wanted to try out. My friend encouraged me to try out for the team, but I refused on the grounds that I was not a strong swimmer, and besides, I didn't have my swimming trunks. In reality, I was threatened significantly by the long swim lanes and the many people who would be watching me struggle in the water. I did not know the proper swimming techniques and I wasn't sure I could swim the length of the pool.

Somehow my friend's gentle persuasions began to raise a small hope in my mind. Maybe making the team was not an impossibility. So I ran home (three blocks), changed my clothes, and ran back, arriving only minutes before my age-group was called to the starting blocks. As I approached the pool, I heard some terrifying instructions. We were to swim fifty yards. That meant I would have to swim the length of the pool twice. As I turned to leave, my friend again encouraged me to try. I took the challenge. Unfortunately, I could swim only twenty-five yards. But no one seemed to care. I was allowed to join the team and improved dramatically as a swimmer that year. I even won a few ribbons and one medal. Changing the threat to a challenge had paid off. I reaped the rewards all summer.

BUILDING ON YOUR CHILD'S STRENGTHS

Discouraging Perfectionism. Children who believe they must be perfect are at a severe disadvantage. Perfectionism is quite paralyzing. It greatly reduces children's willingness to take risks because the consequences of failure seem very high. They drastically overestimate these consequences and thus increase the threatening value of the task. The consequences of giving the wrong answer, falling off a bike, or misspelling one's name are rarely as catastrophic as our children think.

A child is most encouraged when her parents show patience and give permission for less-than-perfect performance. If you're teaching a three-year-old how to color, be prepared for crayon marks outside the lines and a less than economical use of time. Similarly, a teenager balancing his first checking account statement will not necessarily list, total, and calculate all assets and debts correctly on the first attempt. This should be expected and taken in stride. The most encouraging response is, "That's a good start. Let's try it again." Children are not likely to be harmed even by outdistancing their readiness for a task if they can withdraw from the circumstances without facing punishment, loss of love, or fear of disapproval.

We discourage perfectionism when we reward our children's sincere efforts, whether they are completely successful or not. Most parents readily report that they follow this principle, but an inspection of their behavior reveals otherwise. It's easy to *tell* our kids, "Just do the best you can. That's all I expect." But do we really mean it?

The best way to judge whether we really accept less-than-perfect performance from our children is by monitoring how often we allow them to do something that we could do better. Do we insist on zipping up a youngster's coat after his first attempt fails? Do we tell our teenager to step aside and watch Mom when the first sign of cooking inadequacies arise? If we do, we are really communicating that anything less than perfection is worthless. This discourages initiative and clearly implies that the child had better do a task right the first time or refrain from doing it at all.

I regularly hear college students bemoan the fact that

their parents never let them do anything for themselves because they always seemed to do things wrong. Now, away from their parents for the first time, the students live in fear that their unsupervised actions will be viewed negatively by their parents. They are afraid to fail. The sad part is that most of their parents would cringe if they heard these fears. They would plead ignorance of the means they have systematically used to discourage their children.

Most of the time parents who instill perfectionism in this way do so out of impatience. They are more proficient at tasks than their children. It's just easier and less time consuming for the parents to do things for them. I remember when our firstborn was two years old and just learning how to help in the kitchen. My wife made a pitcher of iced tea each day and Kristen wanted to help. Kristen decided that stirring the tea with a wooden spoon was within her skill repertoire and she requested this duty for her personal culinary contribution. The problem? This meant that Kristen had to drag a chair across the floor, situate it in the front of the sink (impeding all other kitchen traffic), and spend about ten times the amount of time it would take Nan to do the stirring. On top of this, Kristen would often spill some of the tea as she sloshed it around. Needless to say, these factors rendered Kristen's assistance a liability.

We had a problem. The solution depended on our frame of reference. If the goal was to expedite completion of beverage preparation, Kristen had just lost a job. But if the goal was to encourage a young child to take on a challenge and learn a skill, kitchen efficiency was inconsequential. My wife determined that encouraging Kristen was the priority goal. She gritted her teeth, and endured the mess, inconvenience, and inefficiency. Sometimes encouraging risk-taking in our children carries a price tag for us.

Corrective Feedback. Unfortunately, all of our children's behavior does not warrant a pat on the back. All children misbehave. As the writer of Proverbs aptly states, "Folly is bound up in the heart of a child" (22:15). We have a responsibility to our children to replace this foolishness with wisdom, and this can only be accomplished through correcting misbehavior.

A detailed discussion of discipline is beyond the scope of this chapter. However, we can encourage our children by giving corrective feedback. This encouragement begins with a *proper attitude*. Corrective feedback must be motivated by a love for our children and a desire to build them up personally. Correction issued merely to shape a child's behavior so that we look good to others is little more than animal training. Offering corrective feedback only when it is convenient for us or when we directly benefit from a change in behavior amounts to selfishness. The most destructive motivation for training children occurs when we guide them into actions solely for our vicarious enjoyment (e.g., pushing your son to become the quarterback you could never be).

The next ground rule for effective corrective feedback is *consistency*. If your child's incorporation of the word *ain't* into her sentence yesterday precipitated some pointers about grammar from you, this verb should be no more acceptable in her speech today. An adolescent's choice of music which was fine with you last night should not be forbidden this morning (though volume adjustment may very well be in order). Consistent feedback is quite productive in conditioning new behavior while inconsistency has just the opposite effect. Psychologists who study reinforcement schedules (consistencies with which rewards and punishments are administered) have found that the variable feedback most deeply ingrains negative behavior.[14] This explains why people will feed hundreds of coins into a slot machine (an inconsistent rewarder), but never put extra money into a soft drink dispenser which doesn't work the first time (usually a consistent rewarder). We must be consistent to be encouraging.

Corrective feedback should be *very specific and given in behavioral terms.* Encouragers point out problems to a child so he easily understands what was wrong and what is needed to get it right. A parent may know what he means when he says, "Shape up, Julie," but teenage Julie may not know what shape her father desires. It is much more profitable to say, "Julie, your actions toward Jim were very demeaning. You were short with him and did not allow him to give his side of the story. Besides failing to listen to him, your tone sounded angry and condescending. He said very little after you ridiculed him at half-time of the game. Did you realize how you were coming across?" Now Julie has a game plan if she wishes to change her communication style.

When giving corrective feedback, be brief and to the point. Lectures which drag on and on are counterproductive and discouraging. Children quickly turn us off when we keep repeating ourselves. And why wouldn't they? Nobody enjoys or profits from being nagged.

Also, be careful to drop a matter once you've dealt with it. Few things are more discouraging to children as having a whole day's worth of misbehavior rehearsed in front of them during supper as one spouse tries to bring the other up to date. And frankly, the spouse receiving the incriminating evidence is rarely thrilled about the presentation either.

Recently my wife and I were reminded of the need to drop a matter after we had corrected the misbehavior of our three-year-old daughter, Anna. A few weeks earlier Anna found a pair of scissors and decided to open her own beauty salon in her bedroom. Since no other customers were available, she volunteered herself for the first haircut. In a matter of minutes she had cut off all her bangs only centimeters from her scalp. Nan, who works diligently to groom the girls, was aghast. When Anna appeared in public, Nan felt obliged to explain the matter to friends lest they think this hairstyle was an ill-fated stab at beauty by my wife. Most of these explanations were fully monitored by Anna, who responded by becoming quiet, holding her head down sheepishly, and hugging her mother's leg. Nan was painfully reminding Anna of her misbehavior repeatedly after correction had been administered. Once she recognized it, Nan terminated this discouraging behavior.

SUMMARY

Parents have a special responsibility to encourage their children early and often. Opportunities for this encouragement present themselves daily, but they can be easily overlooked. Parents must work diligently to recognize these vital windows of opportunity and demonstrate acceptance for their children and their abilities, while building their strengths. No feeling is more nourishing to a child than to feel encouraged by his parents and no prize is more rewarding to parents than to see their child happily growing and learning. Encouragement is the key to this mutual satisfaction.

11.
How Counselors
Use Encouragement

"My mouth would encourage you; comfort from my lips would bring you relief" (Job 16:5).

Ronald consulted me because he struggled with excessive anxiety. He had always been edgy, even as a child. But in the last few years his condition had worsened. Whereas once he felt a bit self-conscious when others were around, now he was scared to be with anyone he did not know very well. His heart would race, his perspiration increased, his ability to concentrate decreased, and he sometimes felt that he would faint if he was not able to escape to a safe place.

As he sat shaking in my office recounting these feelings, Ronald had only one thing in mind. He told me his whole story and then it was time to ask that big question. Ronald paused, fearing that I might give him a negative answer, but then looked me in the eyes and inquired, "Do you think you can help me, Doctor?"

This scene is repeated time and again in the offices of psychologists each day. People struggle with difficulties to no avail and pour out their stories the socially sanctioned healer. Then they ask the question, though not always as desperately as did Ronald, "Can you help me?"

Fortunately, the answer is yes on most occasions, as it was for Ronald. In this chapter we will investigate the use of encouragement in professional psychotherapy. My purpose is not to offer a training manual for counselors, but rather to demonstrate the importance of this vital resource. The same encouragement which professionals rely upon to provide good therapy is available to you for ministering to your friends and acquaintances.

PSYCHOTHERAPY OUTCOME RESEARCH

The study of the psyche is not an exact science and, consequently, there exist numerous theories or schools of psychotherapy. Some practitioners focus on changing one's behavior through use of rewards and punishments, while others extol the importance of gaining insight from the exploration of childhood experiences. There are some therapists who engage in rather nontraditional methods such as primal scream therapy, orgone therapy, and morita therapy. (If you've never heard of these, don't despair; most psychologists could not tell you what a morita therapist is!)

Since such a wide diversity of psychotherapeutic schools abound, the inevitable question arises: Which types of therapy work? Psychologists themselves are keenly interested in this issue and have devoted a great deal of time to its exploration. Because many of the therapies overlap in some aspects, let's look at the common factors in effective psychotherapy.

Research indicates that there are three critical elements of effective psychotherapy: (1) the ability of the therapist to develop a strong and supportive relationship with the client; (2) the ability of the therapist to give the client a new understanding of his difficulties and how to cope; and (3)

Counseling

the engineering of success experiences for the client and his newly found ways of thinking and behaving.[14] Not surprisingly, each of these is a component of encouragement.

An effective counselor must work diligently to create therapeutic relationships with his clients through demonstrating warmth, concern, and empathy. These relationship skills alone tend to encourage the client and boost his morale while allowing him to reduce tension. Helping someone gain a new understanding of his difficulties includes giving him a basis for the distress he's experiencing, identifying his sources of strength, and detailing new options which increase his sense of control. Just learning something about a psychological condition is encouraging to most. Strength and option identification are potent encouragers as well. Encouragement to practice these new behaviors and ways of thinking is always a critical aspect of psychotherapy. We often fear trying new things. Of course, when the risk is taken and success ensues, the encouragement perpetuates itself.

Perhaps the most ardent advocate among psychotherapists of encouragement was the early twentieth century Viennese psychiatrist, Alfred Adler. Adler believed that a major task of life was to move from ineptitude to adequacy. He saw infancy and early childhood as a time in life when we question our personal adequacies. Children must constantly depend on their parents to provide even the most rudimentary resources such as food, clothing, and shelter. They can be prevented from engaging in almost any activity by the more powerful adults and they trust the statements of persons older than themselves, treating their opinions as fact.

In this overpowering world, children may easily develop feelings of inferiority. Adler coined the phrase "inferiority complex" to describe individuals who had deep-seated feelings of inadequacy and powerlessness. Adler believed that children who receive appropriate encouragement develop feelings of adequacy, self-acceptance, and happiness. However, those who are not fed a constant diet of encouragement develop an inferiority complex which has the potential to cause emotional distress for the rest of their lives.

Adler preached the necessity of encouragement in the Austrian school systems and was a very articulate speaker and educator. When dealing with adults in psychotherapy, he championed the technique of encouragement as well. Adler believed that the only way we could help another person overcome early discouragement and inferiority was to help that person understand how his early experiences contributed to his unhappiness. Then we could help that person recognize his personal assets and enhance his self-esteem. Even though investigation of early determinants of behavior is better left to professionals, assistance in strength identification and celebration of successes is very much within the scope of all encouragers

HOPE

Psychotherapy is very much the practice of encouraging hope in people. Hope is a prerequisite to improvement in the emotional arena as it is in the spiritual and physical ones. Hope and its colleague, faith, are discussed extensively in Scripture in reference to spiritual growth and maturity. The entire Christian life is based upon our faith in God, His Son's finished work on Calvary, and our hope in His promises. Christian hope is not blind optimism nor wishful thinking, but is an understanding of the certainty that God will deliver what He promises. We may not understand the method He will use to orchestrate this, however. As such Job could trust God when his family, health, and material resources were taken from him. David could pen psalms about God's protection even when he was a fugitive hunted by King Saul. Persecuted Christians receiving the epistles of Hebrews and Peter could endure their suffering. Paul could say authoritatively that he would be resurrected with a body similar to Christ's. And the Thessalonian believers could stop fretting about deceased brothers and await Christ's second coming. All of these hopes are available to Christians today and can influence our emotional outlook.

Likewise, physical health is affected strongly by our hope. In some very interesting New Testament passages we see the relationship of physical health improvement to hope in even the Great Physician. All the Synoptic Gospels record the events surrounding Jesus' return to His hometown of Nazareth. He taught in the synagogue on the Sabbath and offended His childhood companions. Mark notes, "He could not do any miracles there, except lay His hands on a few sick people and heal them" (Mark 6:5). And Matthew enlightens us that Christ's power was limited there because of the people's lack of faith (Matt. 13:58). Apparently, faith and hope were necessary for healing, even when the perfect cure was present.

Faith and hope play a pivotal role in medical treatments procured through modern medical science as well. Persons suffering with serious maladies succumb to diseases much more quickly when they give up hope. Significant losses often sap hope and contribute to illness and death. For instance, for one year after the death of a marriage partner, the death rate of the remaining spouse is ten times higher than that of other persons the same age. Sick people exercise faith in drugs as well as medical professionals to the extent that placebo medications (pills with no medicinal value) can sometimes produce curative effects.

Encouraging hope is a major concern in the psychological realm. The therapist does not merely dispense a treatment, but is a focal part of the treatment himself. Encouragement developed through a strong personal relationship with his client through active listening and demonstrated caring and support prepare fertile soil for personal investigation and sharing and acts as a catalyst for change.

In the early stages of therapy especially a person borrows heavily from the counselor's store of hope and energy. This is extremely encouraging since the person has often exhausted his personal supply of hope and that of his social support network before initiating therapy. A morale boost is usually the first order of business. The counselor's reassurance that others have suffered with similar problems is usually enough to instill hope and encouragement.

As psychotherapy progresses the instillation of hope remains important, particularly as painful material is investigated and new skills are learned. Progress is often slow and encouragement is necessary to keep plugging away at the problem. Perhaps the greatest encouragement of hope comes as therapy winds down and independence from the counselor is necessary. Similar steps are involved in the encouragement process carried out by nonprofessionals as hope provides energy to blaze a path to improvement.

EXPECTATIONS

In his play *Pygmalion*, George Bernard Shaw insists that a lady and a flower girl differ not by the way they act, but by how they are treated. In *My Fair Lady*, the musical adaptation of Shaw's play, the delightful flower girl Eliza Doolittle expresses these sentiments after she has undergone the transformation from a pauper to a much-praised lady. She contrasts the encouraging style of the sympathetic Colonel Pickering with the unyielding bantering of her tutor, Professor Henry Higgins. Then she concludes that she never ceases to be a lady around the colonel because he never fails to treat her as such, but that Professor Higgins' rough treatment of her prevents her from ever fulfilling the part around him. This is precisely the principle of the self-fulfilling prophecy—sometimes called the Pygmalion effect. According to this concept, merely making a prophecy tends to make it come true.

A number of researchers have demonstrated the effects of self-fulfilling prophecies. In one study which received a good deal of publicity, experimenters manipulated grade school teachers' expectations of students in their classes by randomly assigning school records to students.[15] The unwitting teachers treated the students in accordance to the abilities they *thought* the students possessed, based on the bogus school records. They devoted more attention to the (supposedly) bright students; consequently, these children outperformed their peers in the very same classes. Some teachers even behaved negatively toward those children whose performances exceeded their expectations. This holds true for animals as well. Researchers have shown that laboratory rats do better if the lab technicians are led to believe that they are from a superior breed.[16]

The implications of the Pygmalion effect for psychotherapy are obvious. The counselor's stated belief that his client will overcome his symptoms contributes to his recovery. I believe the opposite is equally true. Care givers who are burned out or disillusioned with their work may very well predict (and subsequently find) deterioration in their clients. I see engendering positive expectations as an integral part of therapy.

Denise was a college freshman who fancied herself unattractive and unappealing. Apparently, she had been an unplanned addition to her family and, as a result, had been fed a constant diet of discouragement about her looks. She was compared unfavorably with her older sisters in personality characteristics as well. Denise fulfilled the prophecy dutifully by giving her face little cosmetic attention, maintaining a bland wardrobe, and shying away from others. In my opinion, she was average in appearance (certainly not ugly), was witty, and had a pleasing personality.

We talked about *My Fair Lady*, and I commented that my job of helping her secure a date was minor compared to Professor Henry Higgins' task of passing off Eliza Doolittle as a lady. (I knew we had 700 single men on campus, some of whom had confided to me that they were having trouble asking for dates.) Denise smiled sheepishly and said, "You know, this is the first time anyone has ever led me to believe I have a chance. Maybe I could go out sometime this year." As you probably guessed, she went out plenty that year, and the other three years she spent at college as well. We worked at length on family and self-esteem issues, but devoted little time to dating after the first few weeks of counseling.

Encouragers must keep their expectations realistic, but should try to see diamonds in the rough. Christians have the advantage of recognizing the power of the Holy Spirit to raise a believer's potential, transform his life, and effect growth. Biblically based "prophecies" of spiritual growth can be made with confidence when a Christian is willing to apply scriptural principles to his life. It is essential, however, that we never imply that this life will necessarily be totally free from suffering or accompanied by great wealth. There is good evidence that these "prophecies" will not come true.

SELF-EXPECTATIONS AND CONTROL

Our positive expectations of others encourage them to expect good things of themselves. Obviously, this is the goal of psychotherapy—helping others function *without* the psychotherapist. Good counselors are in the business of putting themselves out of business with each new person they counsel. I try to instill into my clients realistic expectations which are consistent with their stated needs and teach them skills needed to meet these expectations. When I've done my job well, the person has appropriate self-expectations and can function on his own.

Self-expectations are potent predictors of behavior. It is not uncommon to hear a professional place kicker report that he knew the field goal was going to be good because he had envisioned it even before the snap. Even a weekend golfer can predict which clubs he'll likely hit with accuracy before teeing off. Similar examples in business, education, and Christian ministry abound. When we *believe* we will succeed or fail, we rarely disappoint ourselves.

I often am amazed at the things that bolster our self-expectations of success. After a client of mine had an uncontrollable anxiety attack in public, he became fearful of fainting. I encouraged him to carry a small paper bag with him which he could breathe into to prevent hyperventilation. Armed with a small bag, he expected success and quit worrying needlessly.

I recently ran into a problem in my daily exercise program which threatened my enjoyment of the activity. In reasonable weather, I ride my bicycle into the countryside, exploring the back roads and observing things easily missed from a car. Unfortunately, the inhabitants of rural Indiana are fond of large dogs which, in turn, are fond of chasing middle-age bicyclers. I have an uneasiness about unknown canines which was early instilled into me by my mother (an avowed animal phobic) and which was reinforced by the recent biting of my daughter by a supposedly friendly dog.

On my bike rides I was encountering about two dogs per day on the lonesome country roads. Even though I tried to reason with myself that these dogs were probably harmless, my early conditioning was convincing me otherwise. A predictable pattern arose in my daily excursions: I would enjoy my ride only until I came to the next farmhouse which *might* have a dog. I was hypersensitive until passing that house and all danger faded. But then there was another farmhouse and the cycle recurred. Of course, my uneasiness was quite evident to the dogs who were happy to oblige me by fulfilling my expectations of them.

My self-expectations changed with the purchase of a pocket-size mace spray dispenser. With the addition of this small item, I felt powerful against the dogs. Though I will never use the mace–a dog would have to be a mere foot away to be affected, and even then the wind would have to be blowing in the right direction—I feel secure. Now I can enjoy my bike rides because I expect success in dealing with all the elements of the environment.

Whether aided by a small paper bag, a mace dispenser, a newly learned assertive skill, or a renewed faith in God's plan for our lives, we function much better when we feel in control of our lives. Some of the ways psychotherapists seek to increase their clients' personal control are by helping them gain insights, explore relationships, learn skills, change their thinking patterns, and clarify values. All of these contribute to healthy functioning and are available to nonprofessional encouragers as well. Helping people feel in control of their lives is a tremendous encouragement.

SELF-ESTEEM

Collectively, hope, expectations, and control strongly influence our self-esteem. Self-esteem deficiencies are the most common complaints that bring people in for counseling. Self-esteem is central to emotional well-being and is comprised of two components: a sense of personal worth and a sense of self-confidence. Each plays a role in our psychological functioning and each can be enhanced through Christian encouragement.

The idea that a Christian can experience positive feelings of personal worth is often misunderstood in our religious settings. It can raise some red flags. Some people quickly produce Scripture verses which seem to teach just the opposite. They cite Jesus' words, "If anyone comes to Me and does not hate his father and mother, his wife and children, his brothers and sisters—yes, even his own life—he cannot be My disciple" (Luke 14:26). The Prophet Isaiah proclaimed, "All of us have become like one who is unclean, and all our righteous acts are like filthy rags; we all shrivel up like a leaf, and like the wind our sins sweep us away" (Isa. 64:6).

Indeed, the theological doctrine of man conclusively shows that we are sinners by nature without recourse, except the Lord Jesus Christ. Our hymns reflect the teachings on this basic sinfulness in us. Isaac Watts wrote:

> Alas! And did my Saviour bleed?
> And did my Sov'reign die?
> Would He devote that sacred head
> For such a *worm* as I?

The same sentiments were penned by John Newton in "Amazing Grace."

> Amazing grace—how sweet the sound—
> That saved a *wretch* like me!
> I once was lost but now am found,
> Was blind but now I see.

How can a person like himself when he is a worm and a wretch and performs only filthy works?

On the other hand, there's a wealth of Scripture which shows a very different side of humans. Redeemed persons are said to be a chosen people, a royal priesthood. Peter declares, "But you are a chosen people, a *royal priesthood,* a holy nation, a people belonging to God, that you may declare the praises of Him who called you out of darkness into His wonderful light" (1 Peter 2:9).

Likewise, Paul proclaims believers to be special people called to lofty service. "We are therefore *Christ's ambassa-*

dors, as though God were making His appeal through us. We implore you on Christ's behalf: Be reconciled to God" (2 Cor. 5:20). In Ephesians 1:5 Paul says, "[God] predestined us to be *adopted as His sons* through Jesus Christ, in accordance with His pleasure and will."

Undoubtedly there is a tension in Scripture on the teachings about how people should view themselves. Theologians have wrestled with the issue for years. Some believe that people are totally depraved and should always dislike their human nature. Others decide just the opposite—even though we're sinful in our natural state, redemption changes all that. We should totally like ourselves after our salvation experience.

This issue is of great importance to Christian psychologists because we know that how we perceive ourselves largely determines how we function emotionally. The answer to this dilemma is probably neither total liking nor total abasing of self. Just as in most areas of the Christian life, a balance is required. We do have a sinful nature which is not eradicated when we trust in Christ; to deny this inevitably will lead to pride. However, God chooses us to carry out His programs and empowers us with spiritual gifts and personality characteristics which make us effective ministers for Him. To deny these things leads to self-abasement and ineffectiveness.

We must be willing to look realistically at ourselves—just as God does. We must use what Paul calls "sober judgment" (Rom. 12:3) in appraising ourselves. In this way we can be cautious of the sin nature which still lives within us, but we can also recognize our strengths and spiritual gifts which God wishes for us to cultivate and use in our Christian walk.

Understanding God's acceptance of us can enhance our own self-appraisals and keep them within realistic limits. In reality this is a fundamental way in which God encourages us. Christians with positive perceptions of their worth are encouraged and are very effective for God. Plus, they feel good psychologically.

The other component of self-esteem is self-confidence. This is a belief that we can handle situations which arise in our lives. Self-confident people *expect* to be successful in their endeavors. They are more likely to try new tasks and will persist when they are initially unsuccessful. These are the people who accomplish things.

Just as with personal worthiness, an accurate biblical view must be used when considering self-confidence for the Christian. Total dependence on one's self is unscriptural because it denies our need for God and redemption through Christ. No self-confidence paralyzes us so that we are unable to act either positively or negatively. The balanced view is again indicated. We must recognize that all our powers and abilities ultimately come from God, but He bestows them on us to use as situations present themselves.

The self-confident Christian is effective and productive. He calmly faces life stressors, armed with the belief that God has empowered him to cope successfully. He tries new things, meets new people, and persists in his efforts even when difficulties arise.

God's designs of our personalities through our creation and the early life experiences He allows us to have are ways in which He encourages Christians to develop self-confidence. Further, His spiritual empowerments bolster confidence as we learn to draw on them in times of distress. Believers can encourage one another to develop self-confidence through aiding in the development of personal skills which can be used to cope with situations and telling others when they've done a good job.

People bring self-esteem issues into my office every day. Jan is a typical example. She is in her early 30's, married, and has two young children. Her husband is a business executive and he brings home an adequate salary. Jan decided with her husband that she would devote her time fully to the children, and so she quit her job when their first child was born.

When Jan came to her first session, she was apologetic about even coming in and "taking my time." She reported that she had so many blessings, but she just didn't feel happy. It was as if an ominous cloud always hung over her. Further investigation of her circumstances revealed that Jan was suffering from poor self-esteem. Since she had quit her job, she hadn't felt very productive. She knew that raising her children was an important job, but other women in the neighborhood didn't seem to value that service. She rarely left home to do anything and she always expected failure when she undertook a new project.

Jan's problem wasn't that she had a meaningless job. (Many mothers who work outside the home have poor self-esteem and many mothers who don't work outside the home have positive self-esteem). Jan's problem was that she didn't value herself. She equated gainful employment with personal worthiness. She also lacked self-confidence. She had little faith in her abilities to succeed in anything even though she usually did well at the things she tried. She *knew* that God loved her and that He accepted her, but she didn't know how to transform that into self-acceptance or confidence in her own abilities. Her treatment was a good dose of encouragement. With the help of her husband, we were able to raise her self-esteem level using many of the strategies prescribed in this book.

Karen, a participant in one of my seminars, was married, in her early 40s, and the mother of three school-age children. She worked part-time and reported that her spiritual, family, and work life were satisfying. She had been diagnosed as suffering from a chronic disease and was attending a stress management seminar to learn additional ways to cope with her illness.

The striking characteristic of Karen was her high level of

self-esteem. She accepted and respected herself. She was very self-confident. She was always willing to share personal observations with the other seminar participants and me, and she never hesitated to ask questions when the material was unclear to her. When I taught a new skill, she was usually the first person to practice it in her small subgroup.

Karen was a delightful person. Her self-esteem was evident to all and she was an encouragement to others in the group—even those who had better health than she. In turn, we all encouraged her and she benefited much from the training.

Self-esteem is indeed an important determinant of emotional health. It must be based on the realistic appraisals of God. Encouragement is perhaps the most effective way to build self-esteem. Conversely, persons with high self-esteem are usually the best encouragers. But regardless of self-esteem levels, people thrive on encouragement and use it to build and maintain healthy self-concepts.

Psychotherapy is very much the professional practice of encouragement. Effective counselors are skilled at establishing supportive relationships with people and encouraging them through instilling hope and realistic expectations of success which contribute to positive self-esteem and symptom alleviation. Encouragement is good therapy! But the curative practices of encouragement outlined here are not limited to the professional healer. Indeed, many of the skills are readily available to all caring people who wish to be encouragers.

12.
Is Encouragement Your Ministry?

"And let us consider how we may spur one another on toward love and good deeds. Let us not give up meeting together, as some are in the habit of doing, but let us encourage one another—and all the more as you see the Day approaching" (Hebrews 10:24-25).

"Tychicus is coming! Tychicus is coming!" What welcome words! Excitement filled the air immediately as everyone passed the news on to their friends. And why not? How often did they get a chance like this? It was time to roll out the red carpet and prepare for a blessing. Everyone gathered together and welcomed Tychicus to their fellowship, listening intently to his every word.

Though we have no biblical record of the events surrounding Tychicus' receptions, I suspect this description would be fairly typical. You see, Tychicus was an *encourager*. He was Paul's special envoy, sent often to the early Christians while Paul was in jail.

Tychicus must have been a special person because Paul always links his name with encouragement. To the church at

Ephesus, Paul wrote: "Tychicus, the dear brother and faithful servant in the Lord, will tell you everything, so that you also may know how I am and what I am doing. I am sending him to you for this very purpose, that you may know how we are, and that he may *encourage* you" (Eph. 6:21-22). To the Colossians, Tychicus was described as "a dear brother, a faithful minister and fellow servant in the Lord" whom Paul was sending "that he may *encourage* your hearts" (Col. 4:7-8).

Tychicus was a vital part of Paul's first century evangelistic team as was Barnabas, a man whose name literally means "son of encouragement" (Acts 4:36). Tychicuses and Barnabases are sorely needed in the body of Christ today. Let's look to the Scriptures to discover the particulars of this ministry.

THE PERFECT ENCOURAGER

Imagine yourself as the target of a state-supported terrorist group. You made a public stand for the Lord and demonstrated His power by your strength in proclaiming your faith in hostile circumstances. But, now you've been cited as an enemy of the state and you have moved to the top of the terrorists' hit list. Because no one can be trusted, you have fled by yourself and are holed up in a deserted area without food, water, or any hope of rescue. You're all alone. You wonder whether it's really worth the effort you must exert to stay alive.

If you can hear your own heart pounding and feel the utter despair and loneliness, you have an idea of Elijah's plight as recorded in 1 Kings 19. Queen Jezebel had vowed to kill him and Elijah was terrified. Human options were exhausted. He had nowhere to look except up. It was time to turn fully to the Lord.

We might question Elijah's behavior here since he had

witnessed and performed so many miracles through the strength of the Lord, but God's encouragement is presented clearly to this depressed prophet. First, an angel was sent with bread and water to meet Elijah's physical needs. Soon afterward God dealt directly with Elijah's discouragement by showing him that he was not alone in his struggle—indeed, 7,000 were on his team, fighting the state religion. Beyond that, God gave Elijah a special friend, Elisha, who would accompany the prophet for the rest of his life. What encouragement!

There are many more biblical examples of God's encouragement to His people. Consider Daniel facing hungry lions or his Hebrew friends sentenced to execution in the fiery furnace, and God's timely intercession in each case (Dan. 6:1-24; 3:1-30). However, God is equally encouraging in circumstances which do not seem to have such happy endings. The early deacon, Stephen, was not rescued from his executioners; yet he faced death with a peace and assurance that God's purposes were being fulfilled in his death.

Of course, God is the perfect encourager with unlimited resources at His disposal to use in encouraging others. What can we learn from His encouraging actions?

We have an excellent example of God's encouragement in His Son, Jesus Christ. During Jesus' earthly ministry, He took every opportunity to encourage those with whom He came in contact. He regularly affirmed people for their faith and recognized seemingly small and insignificant acts such as a poor widow contributing to the temple, and children who wanted to sit upon His lap.

Jesus encouraged His disciples routinely, but especially when His death was close at hand. In John 14, Jesus comforted His associates with the familiar words, "Do not let your hearts be troubled. Trust in God; trust also in Me. In My Father's house are many rooms.... I am going there to prepare a place for you" (vv. 1-2). Yet the disciples enjoyed

His personal companionship and encouragement and were very reluctant to see Him go. Later, Jesus promised them another Comforter who would remain with them forever. We know this Comforter as the Holy Spirit—a personal encouragement resource available always to believers.

Jesus used an interesting Greek word to identify His promised replacement. The noun *parakletos* (translated "Counselor" in John 14–16) is made up of two common Greek words: *kaleo*—"to call" and *para*—"around, or along with." The word literally means "one called alongside." It refers to a helper or an intercessor. In its verb form (*parakaleo*) it often means "to encourage, comfort, or cheer up." The work of a *paraklete* is encouragement, exhortation, and consolation. This is the precise ministry of the Holy Spirit in the lives of believers.

Throughout the New Testament *parakaleo* and its derivatives are used to describe God and the Holy Spirit's work with Christians. God is said to grant His children "endurance and encouragement" (Rom. 15:5), and encouragement through appropriate discipline (Heb. 12:4-6). The Holy Spirit "strengthened and encouraged" the church and it grew in numbers and allegiance to God (Acts 9:31).

ENCOURAGEMENT: OUR RESPONSIBILITY TOO

Where does that leave us as Christians? Are we merely to applaud God's work of encouragement? The answer is a resounding no! The New Testament is replete with exhortations commanding us to join God as instruments of His encouragement.

In issuing the duties of believers, the New Testament writers used the same word (*parakaleo*) that was used of the Holy Spirit. God requires Christians to encourage one another daily (Heb. 3:13) and to meet together for this express reason (Heb. 10:25). We are constantly commanded to encourage and build one another up. (Rom. 15:2; Eph. 4:29; 1 Thes. 5:11). We are to encourage the timid (1 Thes. 5:14), encourage others in self-control (Titus 2:6), and encourage each other with the hope of Christ's coming (1 Thes. 4:18).

Some persons develop exceptional encouragement skills and apparently receive special endowments of this resource from the Lord. In Romans 12 encouragement is listed as a spiritual gift for the edification of the body of Christ at large (v. 8). Nevertheless, encouragement is required of *all* Christians even if some have special skills in this area.

If you've ever met a person with the gift of encouragement, you'll never forget him or her. Susie was endowed with a double portion of the gift of encouragement. I met her on my door-to-door sales route while in college. She always welcomed me into her home and seemed genuinely interested in the things going on in my life. She was a good listener and always created an atmosphere which made it comfortable to share experiences with her.

Susie seized every opportunity to reinforce my positive pursuits and this licensed her to offer mild criticism to my problematic behaviors as well. Her exhortations were clearly redemptive and always seasoned with the right amount of salt for a pleasing palate. It was a joy to visit her home—a pleasure to which I frequently availed myself. Interestingly enough, I can never recall a time that she made a purchase from me. Her drawing card to this salesman was her spiritual gift of encouragement.

Conversely, Jenny is not a natural encourager. She is a deeply devoted Christian with a positive testimony in the community. Her natural talents and gifts are in the area of teaching, and this she does with great proficiency. She has the ability to digest passages of the Bible and present them concisely and understandably. She is economical with words, using only as many as are required to convey the material precisely.

Jenny is one of the most capable teachers in her Sunday School. However, she had difficulty filling her classes. She consulted me to discover the reasons for her failure to maintain students. I visited her class and found no problems in the presentation of her lesson. In fact, it was one of the best I had witnessed. But toward the end of the lesson when the comments from the parishioners began to arise, the glitch became obvious. Jenny failed to deal with her students as individuals. She cut off discussions of the students' personal experiences in favor of heady explanations of theology.

Jenny routinely wasted excellent opportunities to encourage her students by failing to acknowledge their experiences and contributions. When this was pointed out to her, she modified her style and allowed more interaction. Now her students became participants. By welcoming their review of personal experiences, little was contributed to the content of her lesson, but personal satisfaction of the participants was enhanced greatly. Jenny learned to encourage her classes even though this was not her strong suit. This simple technique gave her access to many more people and detracted little from her presentations.

PEOPLE ENCOURAGING OTHERS

Biblical examples of personal encouragement abound, especially in the accounts of the early church. It was a much-needed resource due to the persecution regularly encountered by these Christians who sacrificed status and many personal freedoms for the cause of Christ. This encouragement went beyond mere praise for appropriate behavior. Many *parakletes* used encouragement to motivate others to godly behaviors and strengthen their commitments to Christ.

Paul and his colleagues were expert encouragers. Indeed, this became a focal ministry in their missionary journeys.

The Greek verb *parakaleo* occurs repeatedly in the descriptions of these early missionary ventures of evangelism and discipleship. In Acts alone *parakaleo* is used to describe Barnabas encouraging the church in Antioch (11:23); Paul strengthening the disciples in Lystra and Iconium (14:22); the Jerusalem council's encouraging letter to the Gentiles along with Judas and Silas' ministry (15:31-32); the news of Paul and Silas' release from the Philippian jail (16:40); and Paul's "words of encouragement" throughout Macedonia (20:1-2).

But we are not to surmise that encouragement was a one-way street from the apostles to their converts. Paul gleaned a great deal of personal encouragement from his visits to the churches he established and from the letters they sent him. He acknowledged the receipt of this welcomed gift from the Christians in Italy (Acts 28:15), Corinth (2 Cor. 7:13), Phillipi (Phil. 4:10), and Thessalonica (1 Thes. 3:7). Paul clearly enjoyed the reciprocity that godly encouragement always brings from those to whom it is distributed.

ENCOURAGING SCRIPTURAL TRUTHS

Bill is an amazing young man. He can see God's hand in nearly every occurrence, gaining spiritually from seemingly insignificant events. This quality is quite evident in his Bible study. He can read verses that I have read countless times and find an uplifting or instructing truth that never occurred to me. Bill is encouraged regularly by the truths (even the little ones) presented in God's Word.

When we consider encouragement, our minds usually turn immediately to complimenting and praising the actions of others. When warranted, indeed these are very encouraging behaviors. However, encouragement goes beyond these oehaviors. Many biblical truths are encouraging to think about and meditate upon. In fact, *parakaleo* is used in the

New Testament to describe the encouragement and comfort afforded us by God through our spiritual endowments. The Apostle Paul speaks of the "encouragement of the Scriptures" that teach us and provide hope (Rom. 15:4). We are also reminded of our "encouragement from being united in Christ" (Phil. 2:1) and the encouragement in heart from being united with other believers in love (Col. 2:2). Examples of encouraging truths are legion in the Old Testament as well, especially in Psalms where God's character is praised and relied upon for strength and contentment.

Encouraging others with scriptural truths is a very tricky business. Persons often offer these as pat answers or as insincere expressions to others. Funerals seem to be a favorite place to drag out perhaps well-meaning, but very unhelpful responses. How many grieving family members have been subjected to repeated insistences that their departed loved one is "so much better off now" because "to be absent from the body is to be present with the Lord"? Though this sentiment has a clear biblical basis, it is hardly comforting in the initial stages of grieving. Persons trying to encourage mourners with these kinds of condolences usually fail miserably because they do not demonstrate any understanding of the mourner's pain and, worse, they seem to chide the grieving person for failure to be spiritual enough to recognize God's workings.

Almost any biblical reassurance offered without an attempt to understand the feelings of the recipient is counterproductive. Expressing your faith that all things work together for good to those who love God usually will not endear you to the person who recently suffered a financial setback. Even expressions such as "praise the Lord" lose their encouraging potential when used excessively or as comments to every small occurrence.

The context of a remark determines its effectiveness. The recitation of a spiritual truth is appropriate when we understand the feelings of those with whom we are sharing. Funeral home comments such as "I really can't know how you feel right now, but I'm glad that God can understand," are more comforting than those mentioned previously—not because they are more true, just more encouraging. We must strive to present God's encouraging truths in an encouraging way in order to be most helpful.

POINTING OTHERS IN THE RIGHT DIRECTION

The ministry of encouragement is not limited solely to dispensing compliments and reassuring others. There is a strong admonishing component of encouragement which may necessitate confrontation of unhealthy attitudes and behaviors. In the listing of spiritual gifts in Romans 12, many Bible translations render *parakaleo,* "exhortation." This emphasizes the aspect of encouragement which calls for giving honest feedback to others and directing them to righteous and functional behaviors. Being an encourager does not mean we don rose-colored glasses and see only pleasantries. Nor does it promote hypercriticism and finding fault with every action someone takes. Instead, it means that we observe others realistically, praising strengths, recognizing weaknesses, and assisting in the remediation of these deficiencies.

The description of Jesus' ministry in the Gospels demonstrates this balance amply. He complimented persons for their faith, prosocial behaviors, and sincerity in following Him. At the same time He confronted misbehavior, selfishness, and ignorance and set definite plans of action for those who wanted to change. This is repeatedly illustrated in Christ's transactions with His disciples. For instance, in Matthew 16 Peter's confession of Christ is described along with Jesus' strong affirmation of His disciple. But in the same chapter, Peter is rebuked for trying to hinder Christ's sacrifi-

cial death. Jesus recognized that Peter erred through ignorance and followed His confrontation with instructions to
Peter and the rest of His followers on personal self-denial to
mirror His own sacrifice.

Effective encouragers often need to confront inappropriate behavior and attitudes. Indeed, the very fact that others
are misbehaving indicates their need for encouragement.
Ignoring their problems is no more encouraging than blasting
them with a barrage of criticism. They are in need of cheerful
instruction in the proper course to take and of gentle nudg-
ing to get them started toward their goal.

Once when my brother and sister were preschoolers, an
evangelist who was a good friend of my father came to our
house before his meeting that evening in our church. We
lived about six miles from the church and the minister
wanted to drive his car to the service. My father gave him
some directions and then offered little Tim and Kay as
passengers in case further navigation was needed enroute.
My father was reasonably assured that his young charges
knew the often-traveled roads to church. On the way that
evening, the driver became confused and took a wrong turn.
My siblings recognized the error immediately, but responded
only by covering their mouths and giggling to one another.
As a result of this withheld information, the evangelist took
the long and scenic route to church that evening.

Like my silent brother and sister, we often stand by quietly
while others make wrong turns in life. Many times these are
not evidences of misbehavior, but simply the result of ignorance or misunderstandings of life's road signs. Encouragers
recognize confused travelers, point out their errors, and
steer them in the right direction. What could be more
encouraging?

Encouragement is an important ministry which is strongly
mandated and modeled in the Bible. Even though we lack
God's resources to be perfect encouragers, we can use our

abilities and appropriate His resources to assist those in need of encouragement. Biblical encouragement involves recognition of a job well done, confrontation of dysfunctionality, and presentation of a subsequent plan of action when appropriate. Encouragement is the responsibility of every Christian.

Endnotes

[1]Martin E. Seligman, *Helplessness* (San Francisco: Freeman, 1975).

[2]See the following articles:

J. Witmer, C. Rich, R.S. Barcikowski, and I.C. Mague, "Psychosocial Characteristics Mediating the Stress Response: An Exploratory Study," *The Personnel and Guidance Journal* (vol. 62, 1983), pp. 73-77.

The California Department of Mental Health, Office of Prevention, "In Pursuit of Wellness" (San Francisco, 1979).

[3]C. Stout, J. Morrow, E.N. Brandt, Jr., and S. Wolf, "Unusually Low Incidence of Death from Myocardial Infarction," *Journal of the American Medical Association* (vol. 188, 1964), pp. 845-849.

[4]S. Kasl, "Issues in Patient Adherence to Health Care Regimens," *Journal of Human Stress* (vol. 1, 1975), pp. 5-17.

[5]See the following articles:

J.A. Bayton and H.W. Conley, "Duration of Success Background on the Effect of Failure upon Performance," *Journal of General Psychology* (vol. 56, 1957), pp. 179-185.

B. Bernstein, "Extinction as a Function of Frustration Drive and Frustration-Drive Stimulus," *Journal of Experimental Psychology* (vol. 54, 1957), pp. 89-95.

M.M. Berkun, "Factors in the Recovery from Approach-

Avoidance Conflict," *Journal of Experimental Psychology* (vol. 54, 1957), pp. 65-73.

[6]Robert White, "Motivation Reconsidered: The Concept of Competence," *Psychological Review* (vol. 66, 1959), pp. 297-333.

[7]*Op. cit.*, Rosenthal and Fode.

[8]*Op. cit.*, Bayton and Conley, Bernstein and Berkun.

[9]Albert Bandura, "Self-Efficacy Mechanism in Human Agency," *American Psychologist*, (vol. 37, 1982), pp. 122-147.

[10]Mark Knapp, Robert Hooper, and Robert Bell, "I Really Loved Your Article But You Missed Your Deadline," *Psychology Today* (August 1985), pp. 24-28.

[11]*Ibid.*

[12]Rudolf Dreikurs, *Children: The Challenge* (New York: Hawthorn Books, Inc., 1964).

[13]David C. Rimm and John C. Masters, *Behavior Therapy: Techniques and Empirical Findings* (New York: Academic Press, 1974).

[14]See the following:

Jerome Frank, *Persuasion and Healing* (Baltimore: Johns Hopkins Press, 1961).

H.H. Strupp, "Toward a Reformulation of the Psychotherapeutic Influence," *International Journal of Psychiatry* (vol. 11, 1973), pp. 263-327.

[15]R. Rosenthal and L. Jacobson, *Pygmalion in the Classroom* (New York: Holt, Rinehart, and Winston, 1968).

[16]R. Rosenthal and K.L. Fode, "The Effect of Experimenter Bias on the Performance of the Albino Rat," *Behavioral Science*, (vol. 8, 1963), pp. 183-189.

Further Reading

Alfred Adler, *Social Interest: A Challenge to Mankind* (New York: Capricorn Books, 1964).

Alfred Adler, *What Life Should Mean to You* (New York: Blue Ribbon Books, 1931).

Bob Berenson and Robert Carkhuff, *The Sources of Gain in Counseling and Psychotherapy* (New York: Holt, Rinehart & Winston, 1967).

N. Branden, *The Psychology of Self-Esteem* (New York: Bantam Books, 1969).

Ross Campbell, *How to Really Love Your Child* (Wheaton, Illinois: Victor Books, 1979).

Robert Carkhuff, *The Development of Human Resources* (New York: Holt, Rinehart & Winston, 1971).

Rudolf Dreikurs, *Children: The Challenge* (New York: Hawthorn Books, 1964).

Gerald Egan, *The Skilled Helper* (Monterey, California: Brooks/Cole, 1975).

Jerome Frank, *Persuasion and Healing* (Baltimore: Johns Hopkins Press, 1961).

Gene Getz, *Building Up One Another* (Wheaton, Illinois: Victor Books, 1973)

Robert Rosenthal and L. Jacobson, *Pygmalion in the Classroom* (New York: Holt, Rinehart & Winston, 1968).

Martin Seligman, *Helplessness* (San Francisco: Freeman Press, 1975).

Dear Reader:

We would like to know your opinion of **The Healing Art of Encouragement.** Your ideas will help us as we strive to continue offering books that will satisfy your needs and interests.

Send your responses to: **VICTOR BOOKS**
1825 College Avenue
Wheaton, IL 60187

What most influenced your decision to purchase this book?

☐ Front Cover   ☐ Price
☐ Title   ☐ Length
☐ Author   ☐ Subject
☐ Back cover material   ☐ Other:_____

What did you like about this book?

☐ Helped me under-   ☐ Helped me understand
stand myself better   God
☐ Helped me understand   ☐ It was easy to teach
others better   ☐ Author
☐ Helped me understand   ☐ Good reference tool
the Bible

How was this book used?

☐ For my personal reading   ☐ As a reference tool
☐ Studied it in a group situation   ☐ For a church or
☐ Used it to teach a group   school library

If you used this book to teach a group, did you also use the accompanying leader's guide? ☐ YES   ☐ NO

Please indicate your level of interest in reading other Victor Books like this one.

☐ Very interested   ☐ Not very interested
☐ Somewhat interested   ☐ Not at all interested

Please indicate your age.

☐ Under 18 ☐ 25-34 ☐ 45-54
☐ 18-24 ☐ 35-44 ☐ 55 or over

Would you like to receive more information about Victor Books? If so, please fill in your name and address.

NAME: _____

ADDRESS: _____

_____

Do you have additional comments or suggestions regarding Victor Books?